SISTERS ON THE DIAMOND

Published by Bradford House Publishing
Summerville, South Carolina

For more information, sistersonthediamond@gmail.com

Interior Designed by Olivier Darbonville
Edited by Megan Tatreau

ISBN: 979-8-9962523-0-5 (pbk)
ISBN: 979-8-9962523-1-2 (hc)
ISBN: 979-8-9962523-2-9 (ebook)

Sisters on the Diamond

A rookie coach's memoir of grit, grace and unlikely glory.

Crissy Bradford

Dedicated to my family.

To my big sister, Laura: I would have never coached
without you by my side.
Life is better raising our kids together.

To my niece, Riley, for the ongoing encouragement
to finish this book.
Thank you for your texts.
"Have you written another chapter yet, Aunt Crissy?"
Without your reminders, I would never have finished.
You are such an inspiring young lady.

Phillip, Dylan, Amelia:
"I love you the most! I miss you the most!"

Contents

Introduction

I never thought I'd find myself on a dusty baseball diamond, clipboard in hand, coaching a group of six-year-olds with my sister, just two working moms trying to keep up. I've always loved writing and dreamed of authoring books about many other topics—like the string of mom-less boyfriends I somehow picked back to back before finding my husband (seriously, what was I thinking?) or the tightrope of working-mom life, or finding the perfect daycare (does such a thing exist?). Those might still happen someday, but through quiet, unexpected moments, God nudged me toward a different story first: *Sisters on the Diamond.*

Coaching began as a way to make memories with my sister and our boys. Corporate life had me racing between deadlines, work travel, and family time, aching to be there for my kids. Stepping up to coach added to an already hectic load, but I wouldn't trade it for anything; it was one of the best seasons of my life. I didn't expect youth baseball to stretch me so thin some days, but that push was the start of this journey. Coaching with my sister wasn't just about the field; it was the motivation I needed to finally chase my book-writing dream. Coaching had grown into something deeper: a tale of sisterhood, growth, and finding more strength than I knew I had.

Life has a way of handing you "aha" moments, moments where a conviction sets in so heavy on your heart, you can't ignore it. Chatting with my best friend, Lauren, before a long flight to London for work, I grumbled to her about slim pickings for shows to binge watch. "You should watch *Younger*," she recommended. It's a lighthearted series with short episodes starring Hilary Duff (a win for our millennial hearts) and a leading actor who isn't *too bad* to look at. "You'll love it!" she assured me.

I wasn't immediately sold. A rom-com drama about the publishing world didn't sound like my thing, but, Lauren was right. That glimpse into the book world, Hollywood flair and all, lit a spark in me. When I started coaching with my sister, that spark grew into a flame that pushed me to finally chase my book-writing dream.

At the core of it all is our local YMCA. It's not flawless: The fields are patchy, and the schedules can be a mess sometimes. But its heart is pure gold. What we loved about the YMCA is it's a great starting point. It aims to plant values, such as fairness, teamwork, and kindness, in kids that stick long after the last pitch. For that stretch of our lives, it's where we sank our time, energy, and love, building a foundation for our kids. It's the perfect launchpad for young athletes, serving as a stepping stone before the leap to more competitive leagues, or—dare I say—travel teams (we won't get started on *that* debate, though). Every kid deserves a shot at sports, and the YMCA's mix of fun and purpose makes it a haven for families like ours.

I initially set out writing this book as a memento for my family. Through the years of participating in youth sports for my own kids—sometimes simply being a parent, sometimes a volunteer, sometimes cheerleader Aunt Crissy—one pattern emerged: Coaches make a huge impact on their team. Not every coach is going to be amazing every season, and I'd even argue that sometimes having a terrible or apathetic coach helps build character, not only in our young players, but in us. However, there are some fundamental basics volunteer coaches can easily learn to build for a stronger experience within their teams. I hope this story inspires other parents to volunteer, because just as I believe everyone should work in a restaurant at least once in their life, every sport's parent should volunteer coach for a season, or, at the very least, get involved in some way. It's a rite of passage worth taking.

I've heard from many youth parents through the years, and it reinforced the need to get all my thoughts on paper. Maybe, even through the extra work, tears, and excitement of my journey, I can inspire others to volunteer in their kids' youth sports leagues. And not simply volunteer, but dedicate effort into being good at it.

Sports parents—y'all are so fun on those sidelines! You didn't know it at the time, but your stories and sideline conversations kept me writing this book. I've loved getting to know you and your kids, and cheering them on. I hope you enjoy reading this book as much as I enjoy cheering for our kids from the bleachers.

CHAPTER 1

But Are You Any Good?

Standing on the field, right outside the dugout on the first base sideline, I was clinging to my teal clipboard, trying to hide my nerves. I put my head down, quietly exhaled, and thought to myself: *This is it. We're going to lose this game. There goes their undefeated season. They are going to be disappointed.* (An undefeated season meant hibachi versus going to the park for their end-of-season party. They may have only been six-to-seven-year-olds, but they understood what was on the line!)

It was the bottom of the final inning of the game, no more at-bats for us. Bases were loaded, one out. Our team, the YMCA Braves, were up by four runs. Only being up by four and with one out, I knew this was still anyone's game. One of the opposing team's (the Cubs) players got to the plate, and I realized he was a strong batter. I had coached enough games to know this feeling of disappointment; we had a high probability of losing in this scenario. We had before. This was a great team we were playing, and they had several amazing hitters. Sadly, to manage my own expectations, I'd lost hope of winning.

Just then, it began to rain. There was a bit of a chill in the air for a South Carolina May day.

"All right, eyes on the batter, Braves! Know where you're going! You know how to play in the rain!" I shouted, hiding my worry, err… disappointment. The batter hit a pop-up to the pitcher, my nephew, Aiden. We had practiced pop-ups forty, fifty, maybe one hundred times after our bonus practice had ended the previous evening. Catching pop-ups in youth baseball, while difficult, is instrumental to being a winning team. It took me two seasons as a coach to figure that out. It was hit or miss on whether he'd catch it; Aiden had only recently turned eight years old, after all.

The pop fly soared to Aiden. I could feel the entire crowd of families hold their breath… or was that just me? And Aiden CAUGHT THE POP UP.

"AIDEN, THROW TO FIRST!" several parents, including myself, shouted. Aiden, without hesitation, turned to throw the ball to first base for a chance at a double play. I held my breath again; the first baseman, who we called "All-Star Oscar," hadn't been missing catches lately. Oscar CAUGHT THE BALL FOR A DOUBLE PLAY. BRAVES WIN THE GAME!

Without thinking, I ran to the pitcher's mound where Aiden had a huge smile on his face, gave him a hug, lifted him up, and spun him around. I told him, "You just won the game for us, buddy! You just won it for us! WAY TO GO!" I high-fived Oscar, telling him what a great job he did being ready and catching the ball. All the players rushed to the pitcher's mound, circling Aiden, and chanted, "Aiden! Aiden! Aiden!" He stood in the middle of his teammates with a huge smile on his little face, blushing. My sister, Coach Laura, ended up right in there with all our players, fist pumping her arm and cheering on her son.

It was like a scene out of a movie. You'd think Aiden just won the Little League World Series for us. Winning that game was a team effort, and that is a play I will never forget. I could tell that story over and over again (in fact, I do!), and I still get chills every time.

Aiden, and my own little slugger, Dylan, are the number one reason I decided to volunteer to coach—that, and quite a few nudges from God. Creating memories like that one is why I kept coaching after my first season of enduring so many jerk coaches. (I have tried multiple different words to explain these coaches, considering this is meant to be a family book, but *jerk* is the best I can come up with.) Jerk coaches in youth baseball at the YMCA who are *volunteers*? You betcha. It was just as shocking for me, trust me.

Jerk coaches were the ones who bent the rules in their favor—like insisting they were the home team when the schedule listed them as away—called me names to their players (yes, to their six-and-seven-year-olds!), and encouraged shoving my players. Whew—that's barely scratching the surface. I quickly learned I had to know the rules like the back of my hand if I didn't want the coaches taking advantage of me and, more importantly, of my young players. I had to advocate for my players, and I had to advocate for myself.

One day, doom scrolling through the socials as I guiltily admit I sometimes do, I came across the *Pivot* podcast. The podcast host asked Nick Saban, the winningest coach in college football history, if he'd ever coach again. He paused, and then said he'd felt at the end like it might kill him. He only knew one way to do it—all in.

Y'all. I coached six- and seven-year-olds at the YMCA. I am not Nick Saban, but I felt his words in my bones. Because that's exactly how I coached baseball, and I couldn't explain it to anyone without sounding slightly unhinged.

If I'm going to do something, I have to do it 100 percent. This was never so loud and clear to me as when I coached those kids. All the extra bonus practices we put in, arriving thirty minutes early for practice to get more hitting (and for me, pitching practice) in, "You-Tubing" drills, reading blogs, watching other practices, writing the batting line-up, then erasing and starting over. My husband, Phillip, a little on the OCD side, would lecture me about how it's "not smart" to erase pencil in our bed. "Stop erasing, Crissy. Look at all that mess you're leaving in the sheets." I don't think of things like that—he does.

Finally, I invested in a $15 white erase baseball board that hung on the fence outside the dugout each game (I always wrote "Go Braves!" on it—with superstition that if I skipped writing it for a week, we'd lose); my teal clipboard came soon after so I could have Options B-E on extra pieces of paper in the event a player didn't show up (four extra options? Yes. I am not exaggerating).

During the many rides to the baseball fields, my stomach was filled with butterflies. The nerves piled up while I rode in the passenger seat, quietly taking deep breaths. I tried to play it cool for the kids in the back and my husband in the front, not wanting to look like a total dork who cared too much. I failed. And all the while, he and the kids buh-LARED the music in the car while I tried hopelessly to stay in my zone and play it cool. Yes, I cared, I cared a whole lot. While continuing to coach wouldn't have killed me like it could have for Coach Saban, it certainly took a toll on me, and I gained a massive appreciation for coaches.

Plenty of coaches only do it half-heartedly, take short cuts, or just… show up. Not me; I had something to prove—those twelve players, nine of whom were completely random to me, were not going to have a bad experience because they had (gasp!) *women* coaches. They would be glad they had coaches who were sisters, and the parents would not be worried their player wouldn't learn anything *real* about baseball if they were on *my* team.

In May of my third and final season of being head coach for the YMCA Braves Minors, I was on a work trip in New Orleans. Marcie, my colleague, and I were on the same team and were out having lunch with two other colleagues from a different department. We had just found out our team had won three very prestigious design awards. As exciting as it was to share that news with our colleagues, when the topic of my baseball team came up, well, I was glowing more than I was over those awards.

"*You* coach youth baseball?" my colleague asked while raising her eyebrow, then looking around with her eyes bugging out as if she had seen someone running around the restaurant naked. I'm no mind reader, but I feel pretty confident she was thinking: *Girl, you are crazy*. (I know I'm short, standing only five-foot-nothing, and, admittedly, a little stocky… but did I seem *that* incapable? Sigh. Yet, she was not the first and certainly not the last to give me a similar look when I shared I coached youth baseball.)

"Yes, I coach! My sister is my assistant coach, and both our boys are on our team. It's a lot of fun, it has challenging moments, but it's been very rewarding."

She paused for a moment. "… but are you any good?"

I couldn't help but smile, not the least bit offended. In fact, I appreciated the question, maybe because I had the perfect answer. As I paused before I answered, Marcie chimed in, "Oh yes, she's very good—they win a lot!"

My smile grew. I looked her dead in the eyes, and said confidently and calmly while slowly nodding my head, "I'm *very* good."

I proceeded to tell her this was my third season. I explained I was a "super sponge." I soaked up all the wonderful traits about the coaches I watched and admired and made sure to avoid the nasty traits. This resulted in some wins in my second season, but still some losses. I was hopeful to achieve my goal of being undefeated this season—a tough one, but not impossible.

I've always been extraordinarily career driven. Over the last eight years of being a mother, I sometimes questioned how my corporate ambition fit into this season of life. I've always had a mission for my family—to continue building generational wealth—which means leaving my job wasn't a part of the plan for us. I'm competitive at heart and cannot wish or pray it away. It's how I'm wired. I've found a level of success in the corporate world, one I'm proud of, even as my ambition keeps nudging me forward. So coaching became the most wonderful passion and gave my brain a break from work and real-world worry. When I was out on that field, I was focused only on coaching. It came with a huge amount of heartache and growth, but so much fun and immense reward. While those three AMAZING design awards were exciting for me, it's no wonder that coaching baseball is what lit me up that day during our lunch conversation.

CHAPTER 2

Sisters Who Coach Together, Stay Best Friends Forever

"Some of these kids have literally never thrown a ball before!" Laura exclaimed, still catching her breath after our first practice had ended and all the kids had left. She was at the catch-and-throw station and had to chase multiple overthrows across the dirt and grass field.

I had looked at her station sporadically during that first practice, watching her run and chase after the ball when players would overthrow (which was pretty much every rep), and there were times I remember thinking, *What is she doing out there?*

But I felt the exact same: All those parents' eyes were judging us, wondering if we had any clue how to teach their kids to throw straight.

Practices were often a little wild like that. Time went by so fast in the short one-hour that we had, especially in the first season when there was so much to teach each of the players.

I remember early on in one of our practices sternly calling out to Laura: "Two more minutes, Coach!" I was alerting her we needed to let the kids get a drink of water, and then rotate stations.

I received no acknowledgement. Coach Laura just kept pitching balls in her hitting station, zeroed in on the batter. Meanwhile, the other kids in her station were supposed to be fielding the balls and instead were poking each other and giggling.

Two minutes passed by, and Laura was still out there pitching balls to her station. "COACH LAURA," I said louder, "TIME TO ROTATE STATIONS!" Laura often needed to go over the allotted times for our stations; she was insistent on ensuring the weaker hitters got to hit the ball and didn't just miss every swing. She came to the dugout with her kids for a sip of water and said breathlessly, "Man, time goes by quick out there! Whew." She took a sip of her water, then said, "All right, let's get back out there!"

We quickly learned to keep an eye on our watches during station and practice times. We wanted to get in twenty to thirty minutes of scrimmaging toward the end of practice because the kids loved it and we loved it. Practices go by a lot faster when you are coaching versus a parent sitting on the sidelines.

Eventually, our insecurities wore off, Laura mastered the "T" method for wild throwers, and I stopped worrying so much about going over our time; I learned to pivot more in the moment.

From the first time I stood on the pitcher's mound with my hands trembling during my first few pitches, to the games where I held it together just long enough to make it to my car before letting the tears fall, it became clear I was meant to spend this time with Laura, coaching our sons on the ol' ballfield. Through every second of it, Coach Laura and I knew we were building lifelong memories.

"It's what we'll talk about when we're sitting in our rocking chairs, old and gray," she'd often say.

Laura is a tall, thin, athletic almost-forty-year-old brunette, who I had running around like a chicken with her head cut off, herding the kids as if they were an energetic group of twelve puppies who just wanted to wrestle, play in the dirt, and go every which way *except* the way Laura wanted them to go. She's always been the active type, buzzing with energy.

She's a part-time physical therapist at a nursing home for very old people who have limited mobility, so she basically teaches them to wipe their own butts so they can live out the rest of their days independently, getting on and off the toilet with a little dignity. She'd never put it that bluntly, though, and often corrects me: "It's a *skilled nursing facility*, Cris!"

But we're able to laugh about her job—you have to, considering the gravity of what she's carried through the years. There was the sweet patient she adored, who always asked Laura how our baseball lessons were going and cheered us on, until one day, she wasn't there anymore. And then there was the grumpy patient who griped about everything, from too much peanut butter on her PB&J to Laura's therapy sessions, only to blame Laura and the nurse after she tumbled out of bed, ignoring every bit of their advice. Here is your warning: Take your physical therapists seriously as you age, folks.

Laura and I agree on a lot—not everything, but a lot. We had similar childhoods growing up but different teen years. Our parents are divorced and separated when I was eleven and she was thirteen. Most years until we got to college, we didn't like each other a whole lot, or at all, probably. People seem pretty surprised by that now if they didn't know us then.

I was the type of little sister who eavesdropped on Laura's phone calls with her high school sweetheart, her now-husband of fifteen years. She wouldn't let me pick the music in the car. I stole her clothes. She stole the chocolate chip cookie dough chunks out of my ice cream. You know, sister stuff. Now, Laura is my very definition of ride or die.

Yes, there were many days when you could catch either of our husbands saying things like:

"Crissy, your sister is the worst dugout coach, OK? Those kids do not sit on the bench, they do not line up when it's time to line up for their at-bat."

"Laura needs to get those kids in the outfield to pay attention, Crissy!"

"Laura! Who is up at bat? The entire crowd is waiting…"

"I'm *TRYING!*" she'd learn to fire back, insisting the six-year-old attention spans were the problem and not *her* attempt at coaching.

As a biased party, I never did see it as her fault. To be honest, outside of me pitching every inning, I thought her job was tougher than mine. I had more baseball wherewithal, so I directed and strategized; she had to manage the puppy chaos. And herding for the first two seasons was an extreme sport in and of itself.

I'm lucky I got to coach with my sister, someone who I didn't have to worry about "bossing around"—I enjoyed telling *her* what to do for once (Little sister syndrome? Who, me?). She was a great listener, and she didn't question me—she just did what I asked.

Coach Laura rallied the troops when they were down and out. She repeated herself twenty times over to remind the outfielders where they were going if the ball came to them. And to "RUN! RUN and CHASE the ball!" She'd scream in the player's ear, while flailing her arms in the direction of the ball, as she jogged next to the player, hurrying him along to where he needed to go.

She came early to practice and left late with me. Our husbands would text us wondering how late dinner would be because they knew we were chatting late in the parking lot. She practiced on weekends with our kids, even if I couldn't make it. She thought of drills, and lugged equipment to and from her house. She explained the game to the players so they wouldn't make the same mistake twice. She ran my youngest to the bathroom so I could keep pitching to the players. She managed all the boo-boos and accidents while I kept practice running. She toasted me on big wins and let me vent when we found out one of the coaches called me "sassy" to his team. In the heat of the game, she'd walk up to me and say, "Cris, look over there at all our players' parents—they all have your back, whatever call you think is best." She cussed like a sailor behind the scenes about the coach who made me question everything, who had me in tears at the end of our first tournament. She reminded me he was a moron and everyone knew it. She brought a change of clothes for the Dunk Your Coach YMCA fundraiser, knowing she'd need to step in after I was dunked twenty times in the 50-degree weather. (Coaching the "T"-method drill in practice really paid off—their aim was on-point during that season two fundraiser!)

She was the best assistant coach I could have ever asked for, and, if it wasn't for her, I would have never coached, and we would have never become a victorious team. We were the sisters who coached together—the ones with the reputation to have a blast and to win.

Laura was more than right: Coaching with her is definitely what we will be talking about in our rocking chairs when we are old and gray.

CHAPTER 3

"Put My Time In"

I *never* pictured myself as a coach, until God threw me a curveball named Aiden and a storm of signs I couldn't dodge. My nephew, a scrawny six-year-old blondie, was shrinking on his YMCA soccer team. He was benched too often for a kids' league and too shy to shine among strangers. I'd watch him shuffle around, lost in the swarm, and think, *This kid's a baseball player.* He had that little-slugger swagger, even if he didn't know it yet. Soccer was fine—it's great exercise—but baseball offered personal turf, one-on-one with the ball. I had a hunch he'd thrive there, and spoiler alert: He did.

My niece, Riley, on the other hand, was a different breed, fierce, fearless, and naturally talented at anything involving a ball. At nine years old, she was already juggling soccer, basketball, and volleyball, giving us a glimpse of the all-star she was bound to become. Watching her and Aiden play was one of Phillip's and my favorite weekend activities. Our own kids weren't quite there yet. At the time, Amelia was two, and Dylan was five, still in the "micro soccer and tee ball chaos" phase. If you've never watched two-to-four-year-olds play sports, let me paint the picture: They run in random directions, trip over their own feet, and generally look like a bunch of overexcited puppies. Hilarious? Yes. A real sport? Debatable.

So, "Why not just be the Dugout Mom? Why didn't Phillip coach? Why didn't he at least pitch?" I suppose they are fair questions, especially considering how ragged I ran myself some days and the fact that Phillip is an absolute natural at sports. He is the kind of person who can bet on just about anything and somehow walk away a winner, much to the groans of our friends. High school basketball, pickup football, random backyard competitions—it rarely matters. Baseball is no exception. He played for a year in high school and probably crushed it, too, but his heart has always lived on the basketball court.

That first season, though, coaching a group of six-year-olds was not his thing yet. At the time, he was happily knee deep in Flesh and Blood card game nights two or three evenings a week, and he was not quite ready to trade that world in for dugouts, dirt, and wrangling small humans with oversized helmets.

Me? I wanted it.

"Why sit in the stands when you can run the show?" Phillip would say to me, grinning, complete with his sweet little wink I can't resist. "This could be your Flesh and Blood card game. A pastime that takes your mind off everything except the game."

So, while he was on toddler duty chasing our two-year-old tornado, Amelia, around the bleachers, I decided to hit the mound. He may not have been in the dugout (well, we may have had to kick him out a few times), but his sports smarts became my secret weapon. Not that I'd ever admit that to his very handsome but smug face.

The signs kept piling up. Take Dylan, my five-year-old slugger. He'd ruled two seasons of tee ball, whacking my backyard pitches like a mini pro. Another year of him chasing toddlers around bases felt like a snoozefest to all of us; we could tell he needed more. Bumping him up to play with Aiden made sense. Phillip told me in agreement, "He'll hold his own with you out there, Crissy." Then, my sister was locked in as assistant coach, which was perfect, because who else could I trust to wrangle this chaos with me? God was starting to make it all come together.

Work threw in a nudge, too. Every year, my corporate job commits to Impact Month, a company-wide focus on community service. The initiative actually began with my boss, Alvin.

That first year, the project I chose was a virtual career day for kindergarteners. It was sweet enough. I sat in a VR headset explaining restaurant training and career paths to wide-eyed kids for about thirty minutes. It mattered, but it also ended quickly. When it was over, I immediately wanted to do more in my own community, something that lasted longer than a scheduled call on my calendar.

I also knew I would have Alvin's support if I committed to coaching and needed to leave work once a week to get to the field early and set up for practice. He had supported me throughout my career, and this was no different.

That is when the YMCA's constant plea for coaches started ringing louder in my head: Put your time in now, while they are young and while you're able to handle it (before they get too strong and hard at hitting). I thought about it more than I expected to.

Then there was Coach Jess from Dylan's tee ball days. She was a rockstar—outgoing, unflappable, making it look effortless. She ordered custom shirts for the kids and handed them out at an end-of-season party at her house, complete with a jump castle and homemade gumbo. For tee ball! That's next-level effort for a league where scores barely matter and kids just run in circles. I figured coach pitch would be the same vibe—fun, innocent, with a small step up. Was it naïve of me to think that? Yes, 100 percent. It's hilarious to think back on it now, but her spark helped light my fuse, as naïve and misplaced as it may have been.

I'm an introvert. I can be outgoing when I need to be, but I felt it was time to expand my circle instead of leaning only on Laura. Coaching promised new faces for one season, a chance to step out and serve. Toss in my high school cheerleading and softball pitching days, and I thought, *I can yell, I can pitch overhand with practice. Herding six-year-olds? I got this.* God was chuckling from above, y'all.

I prayed about it at night, half expecting the answer to be no. Instead, what I felt was simple and steady: Give it a try. *Just one season*, I told myself. *Put my time in.* That is what I told everyone else, too. Famous last words. I had no idea what I was getting into… did I mention that already?

Phillip would eventually take this age group on himself and ended up coaching for two seasons after I wrapped up my final year; he did a great job. But at the time, before I had lived it, before I had survived it, this league felt like jumping straight into the deep end. Many would argue this is the hardest league to coach. If it sounds like I'm patting myself on the back, I am! Coaching six- and seven-year-olds is no joke.

They're strong enough to hit the ball hard, but they have absolutely no idea what to do with it afterward. Every single play requires a real-time, step-by-step breakdown. Where to run. Where to throw. Who to throw to. And all of it happens while the ball is already rolling and the clock is ticking.

"Crab walk!"

"Gator chomp!"

"At least try to stop the ball with your body!"

"Look where you're throwing. No, not there. First base. FIRST. You're the runner. Don't field the ball. Keep running!"

That is what coaching six- and seven-year-olds sounds like in real time. And it throws off even the most experienced coaches. One day, a coach who had coached kid pitch pulled me aside. He looked at me completely seriously and said, "This is one of the hardest things I've ever done in my life." Let that sink in. Coaching coach pitch minors **was harder** than coaching older kids who are learning how to pitch the ball.

The greatest part about this is I found out he was an assistant principal at a local high school. A man who spends his days navigating hormonal, attitude-filled, teen chaos told me this was harder. I laughed when I found out. Teen years are objectively the hardest phase of life. I would not go back even if someone paid me a billion dollars. So, yes, absolutely I give myself major kudos for putting my time in with this age group.

Now, don't get me wrong. I'm not saying this to scare off future volunteer coaches. Quite the opposite. If you're reading this and thinking, *I kind of want to try this*, you absolutely should. Like the old saying goes: "Nothing worth having comes easy." Or, as Teddy Roosevelt put it: "Nothing in the world is worth having or worth doing unless it means effort, pain, difficulty."

"One Season, I Swear."

Going into season two, I had no intention of coaching again. None. Zero. Zip. The way season one had ended had me done.

And yet… my husband, my sister, and, I'm fairly confident, some of the amazing parents from my team conspired to drag me back. (Looking at you, Phillip.)

And, honestly? It was for the best.

God's nudges came with a catch. Before I got to the point of realizing this was one of the best experiences of my life, it was a trial by fire, starting with coaches who'd twist rules like they were playing for the World Series. I'd need every ounce of faith, grit, and Phillip's sideline savvy to fight through it.

CHAPTER 4

Season One

My First Coaches' Meeting

You could cut the tension with a knife walking into the gymnasium for my first coaches' meeting. The gym itself didn't help. There were very few windows, so everything was bathed in that dull, yellow gym lighting that makes even a normal conversation feel serious. The chairs were arranged in a wide oval, open in the middle, with David, the new YMCA sports director, standing at the front and the rest of us curved around him.

What strikes me most now was how quiet it was. Later coach meetings would have kids off to the side playing video games or coloring on the floor, background noise softening the edges of whatever tension was in the room. But that first meeting had no kids. No distractions. Just grown adults sitting still, waiting.

At the time, I wasn't a source of the tension. I didn't yet know enough to be. In later seasons, I would absolutely become a point of friction for a couple of coaches, and by then I'd be grateful to have a coach buddy sitting next to me. But that night, I was taking it all in, wide-eyed and unaware of what I was stepping into. I remember telling Laura afterward what a strange, intense vibe it was, but genuinely not thinking too much of it.

Because here I come, all excited to be volunteering, just naïve as can be, a little shy, but thinking I might make some coach friends. I even tried to look the part, wearing sporty clothes, but with my makeup done and hair styled in curly waves, so I made a good first impression. HAHA. Coach friends? What are those? Of course, I am kidding. My husband and I have made a lot of coach friends since that meeting, but it's laughable looking back now because I thought it would be easier to make them.

What I didn't realize yet was that coach relationships are friendly right up until they aren't. One minute everyone's smiling, the next minute you're wondering if you accidentally walked into a rivalry you didn't know existed. And, yes, that applies to youth baseball, too.

David, or "Coach David" as my kids still call him, is good at what he does. He still runs impactful developmental camps during the summer and fall, and he's one of those steady presences families quietly rely on without realizing it. He's a single dad to his son, Camden, who becomes a part of this story, too, and you can tell immediately being a dad is his first and most important job. David looks exactly like the sports director you picture in your head: bald, blue-eyed, and always dressed like he just came from or was heading to a game. He wears a lot of purple, leftovers from his Illinois days, where he coached and where his son earned some baseball accolades in high school.

What mattered most to me, though, was how David showed up in that first season. Since it was his first year directing the baseball program, I kept that in mind and reminded myself of it often. I reminded Coach Laura. I reminded parents. New director. New systems. New expectations.

David's instinct was to keep the peace, sometimes to a fault. In that first season, his diplomacy rubbed some of us the wrong way, especially in moments where clarity or firmness might have helped. At the time, I chalked it up to him being new, still finding his footing. And for the most part, that steady, even-keeled approach served him well.

I had no idea what the program looked like before David. I didn't know the previous director's style, the rules he enforced loosely or tightly, or how much freedom he gave coaches. That baseline mattered, because it quickly became clear that whatever had existed before had caused some friction.

I say that because clearly the rules the season before had something to do with the tension in the gym during that meeting. There were probably around twelve to fifteen coaches in there, one other mom coach, and all the rest were men. I remember that so well because one—the woman coach was the most outspoken coach in the meeting, and two—she stopped coaching after that season.

There were times I thought being able to talk to her would have been helpful, but in hindsight, maybe not. In the meeting, I remember thinking, *I can't believe how sour she is acting. It's not a good look… it's not that serious.* She was bumping up from coach pitch majors to kid pitch, so a lot of her opinions and questions didn't pertain to me. At the time, she was in a completely different world, but one I would soon enter.

David handled that meeting calmly. He didn't over-explain. He didn't lecture. He handed us the rulebooks, rosters, background check paperwork, and team requests, then walked through the rules at a high level.

In this league, players could request their coach, and the coaches could pick their players—there's no skill assessment or evaluations like other leagues have. There are pros and cons to not having evals, but in a beginner's league like at the YMCA, one pro is that kids at a young age trying out a new sport tend to have more fun when they are comfortable around kids they already know. At the Y, you are surrounded by kids of different skill levels and not likely to be the only kid who hasn't played before. There's cons, too, which I won't get into right now. It will come out, you'll see. We are lucky to live in a small city where there are multiple options for leagues with different rules. It's nice to try out what you like and aim to put your kid where their skills and personality will fit best.

David said he would bring the fence in a bit so the players could hit some dingers (baseball term for home runs). At the time, I didn't realize how controversial something as simple as a fence could be. I would learn quickly people had strong opinions about making the game easier for kids, especially when it came to home runs. Home runs are extremely exciting for the teams and give the players a goal to work toward.

The opposing argument for bringing the fence in is you can't make it too easy for the kids to hit home runs because you don't want them to think it's simple; additionally, some teams naturally hit more dingers than the others. (My take is to accept the challenge and work more on hitting. I say this having only one of my players making a home run during a game. Mostly, we had a few boys hit it over the fence in practice, but it took **three seasons** to get them to that point. Only two players on other teams in my league hit dingers in my third season, and I am thrilled for them and their coaches. What I came to believe, after watching season after season for this age group, is giving kids a chance to experience success early doesn't cheapen the game. It keeps them in it.)

David talked about having a catcher and how he was required to hand out the catcher's equipment; in coach pitch minors (my league) and above, the catcher needed to have the gear on (I quickly learned this was quite lenient). Some players, in my experience, love being the catcher and want to wear the equipment. But it's SUCH a nuisance for a five-year-old to put on catcher's gear in 90-degree South Carolina heat for an inning they won't *actually* play. The catcher's gear often sat in the back of my white Honda Pilot for weeks on end without being touched. It annoyed my OCD husband terribly.

David talked about reps. He *always* talked about reps. And he was 1000 percent right about reps. He said to get your players in three to four stations per practice and get other parents involved. Do not have these young kids standing around to build sandcastles in the dirt or pick the grass out of the field. Reps. Reps. Reps. "If you scrimmage the whole practice," he said, "then they will never make any plays because they are not learning the fundamentals." This stuck with me. I made a mental note to myself: Google drill ideas for Little League. (If it were now, I would ask my favorite AI chatbot instead—boy, the tricks I could have learned quicker if AI was where it is now, back then.)

He talked about pitching. This was a key moment for me. He emphasized not being prideful and to move up a few steps and pitch the ball. He said no one wants to be the reason a player strikes out, so get the balls over the plate. "Don't worry about where the pitcher's rubber is in coach pitch," he said. "Just get the ball over the plate. If these players don't hit, then there is no game." He also mentioned we should all try to take a knee when pitching so we're at a good level for the players. Don't forget! I'm already only five feet tall, much lower to the ground than the other coaches. He said **absolutely no underhand**. I pitched in softball, so I thought underhand would be easier to pick up. *Guess I need to get my own reps in for overhand pitching*, I thought to myself.

I got my roster, my sweet, little roster including Dylan, Aiden, Aaron, and Oscar. My son and nephew, my sister's neighbor (Aaron), and one of Aiden's friends from his class, Oscar (at the time, we had no clue he was going to be such an all-star). The rest of the roster would be filled with "free agents." Free agents are players who did not make a request for any particular coach, and who could match my practice day and time, Wednesdays at 5:30 p.m. By the way, I didn't know what to think of these kids. The most I knew about my roster was that my son could hit most of the time when I pitched to him, and he fielded the ball OK for a five-year-old. I had no clue how Aiden would *actually* play, just that I had an intuition he had the swagger of a baseball player.

After the meeting, I talked to David outside. "David, it's my first season coaching," I told him. "My son is five, and my nephew is six and a half. Do you think we are all good to bump my son up to play coach pitch? I don't know what to expect."

Looking back, I am pretty sure he gave me a bit of a look, like, *This woman has no clue what she is getting into*. I made sure to work in that I played softball, so I was not starting at ground zero. I also mentioned my son could hit when I pitched to him, so I didn't want tee ball to bore him.

David reassured me bumping him up was the right move and reiterated to me one on one that getting him hitting was going to make the biggest difference in the game. **If the players don't hit, there is no game.** I've now said this so many times, it's hard to remember David was the one who initially told me this. But it's important to note he gave me all the same tools he gives everyone else; the difference is what Coach Laura and I did with those tools.

Later that season, I would see another side of David, not just as a director, but as the adult responsible for dozens of children in a crisis. One afternoon, during a perfectly ordinary practice, in the middle of my first season coaching, no less, I learned just how seriously David took the safety of these kids. We were on the back field of the complex, tucked away from everything else. We felt pleasantly isolated, almost in our own little baseball world. Laura and I had just started fielding drills when David rolled up in his John Deere cart.

He didn't raise his voice. He didn't panic. He simply stepped off the cart, walked straight to me, and said under his breath, "I need everyone to walk to the gym immediately and get out of this area. Start moving now. I'll follow you." For a split second, my brain stalled. *Grab bags? Grab bats? Drive? Walk?*

"Leave the cars," he added quietly. "Head to the gym parking lot. You won't be able to leave the complex. There's an active shooter in the area."

The words landed like a weight in my chest.

I turned to the parents and players and did exactly what came to mind—stay calm and move fast.

"OK, everyone, we need to head to the gym parking lot right now. Let's move quickly."

As we started toward the building, we heard shots. Not close enough to see anything, but close enough that every one of us understood this was real. That was when we picked up the pace.

I took inventory in my head: my son, Laura and Aiden, every player, siblings, parents. I grabbed the hands of the slower kids, and, in a couple of cases, scooped up the littlest ones who couldn't keep up. We moved as quickly as we could without causing chaos.

As we passed the end of the road, blue lights flashed in the distance.

Once we got inside the gym, Laura immediately started texting parents who were running late: "Don't come. Active shooter in the area. We're all OK."

We were a bit shaken, quiet, wide-eyed, but we were safe. We waited upstairs in the playroom for hours, kids sprawled across the floor with toys and the snacks we could scramble together, parents huddled, trying to smile for the kids. Eventually, around 8:00 p.m., we were cleared to leave.

Later, we would learn the shooter hadn't been targeting the YMCA. He had robbed a local store nearby and used the complex as part of his escape route.

In the days that followed, several parents told us how grateful they were for how David and the YMCA handled this situation— calm, clear, fast, and decisive. And I understood, in a deeper way than any rulebook could have taught me, that this league was about more than baseball.

But "bigger than baseball" and "keeping twelve six-year-olds focused on a field" are two different kinds of challenges.

Our First Practice

Regardless of how prepared I tried to be, I was still a bag of nerves during our first practice. Although I am writing this a few years later, the thoughts that ran through my head during that practice on that patchy, grassy, barely-a-baseball-field are as clear as day. *Am I being too serious? Am I not being serious enough? Do*

I look ridiculous? Do they think I'm favoring my son and nephew? Do they think I'm not giving their child enough attention? Do they think I don't know what I'm doing? (Because they'd be right!) Are they bummed we are women? Am I going to get this ball over the plate when pitching?

One reason we love the YMCA is because of the values they aim to instill in their programs. While "The Y" may not be the most competitive league in your city, at least you know your player is going to become part of a team. That's the YMCA's goal, anyway. In the handbook for coaches, it explains you should huddle with your team before every practice and go over a value like "good sportsmanship," "giving," or "helping others." Admittedly, I didn't keep up with this every practice of every season, but it did give me an excellent foundation on the **importance of a huddle.**

We started each practice with a huddle. I cannot remember what value we discussed at the first practice, but I vividly remember all of the kids introducing themselves. Coach Laura has a curiosity about people, so she had a great idea to have the kids go around and say their names, grades, what school they were in, and their favorite thing. This was great because we got a glimpse into each of their little personalities, and, also, I got to start learning their names! That was another reason I was nervous: *How am I going to remember all their names?*

As the kids went around the circle, little patterns started to emerge. A couple of them were homeschooled, which I thought was pretty cool. There were two girls on the roster, and I remember feeling hopeful about that. I was coaching with my sister. We were women out there running a team. Surely this would inspire them. Spoiler alert: It did not.

To be fair, they were lovely girls, just not the ones for baseball/softball. One of them quit halfway through the season, and the other barely made it through. And that was a lesson for me early on. You can show up with all the right intentions, but not every kid is meant to stay.

A few kids already knew each other from school and even shared the same classroom (hooray for this!); it felt like a small win for team chemistry. I also realized my roster skewed young, with several five-year-olds, including Dylan and Aaron, and another one who would join us at the second practice. One of them, our sweet and focused Theo, would stay on our team until he aged up.

I also learned I was going to mix up names. Two boys blended together in my head those first few weeks. Same size, similar skill level, completely different kids. It's funny now because they look nothing alike, but, at the time, my brain could not keep them straight. That's something I emphasize in my playbook (Chapter 11): Learn their names early—you will need to use them often.

One moment from that first huddle stayed with me. One boy spoke very softly when it was his turn. He paused with extreme shyness before sharing his name and grade, and when he finally did, I felt a rush of excitement for him. That pride only grew as the season went on and his confidence flourished. Every kid shows up to the field carrying something different, and watching them find their footing is part of what makes youth baseball so powerful.

When the huddle ended, it hit me: Every. Single. Player was new to coach pitch. Only a handful had any tee ball experience. I was still learning, too, and I hadn't yet grasped how big the leap from tee ball was. I thought we were just taking a small step up.

Game One

27-3. Yeah, OK, I totally made that score up. However, the opposing coach's daughter from this game ended up playing on my team—Coach B, the same coach (the high school assistant principal) who said coaching this age was the toughest thing he's ever done. And we've remained friendly, so I am willing to bet he'd agree the score of this game was somewhere in the ballpark of 27-3—I am likely being generous giving him three runs.

That first game, as lopsided as the score was in our favor, was not without its trials. I overthought the rules in a big way. I had one or two extra players, and the rulebook said they had to sit out, but for no longer than two innings. If they sat for the field, they had to sit for batting, too. Trying to follow the rules exactly as written, I did what seemed logical at the time. I made multiple batting line-ups. I was determined to do it "right."

This is astronomically embarrassing to admit now.

While I was out on the mound pitching, trying to keep balls over the plate and kids focused, one of the dads approached Coach Laura. His tone was sharp. Frustrated. The kind of criticism that comes out when someone assumes you don't know what you're doing. Phillip would later say it was somewhat warranted. That dad didn't know us yet. But the way it felt to me at the time, there was already a stigma attached to us. Two women coaching. New. Rookie mistakes. The doubt came out before the understanding.

Once Phillip saw how the conversation was unfolding, he stepped in to help Laura resolve it. That mattered more to me than anything. I trusted both of them, so when Laura came to me and said we needed to put the player in, I didn't question it. I could tell from her face that something had gone sideways, and I fixed it immediately. The player went in. The situation cooled down. Later, the dad apologized. Over time, we built a great relationship with him and his family. But, in that moment, it stung.

Later that day, Phillip laughed and said, "You just put all the kids in an ongoing batting line-up, Crissy." (You know, in a "duh" kind of way.) And I took it. Because he wasn't wrong. I was trying so hard to follow the rules, I missed the forest for the trees.

What makes this moment quietly vindicating is that years later, when Phillip started coaching himself, he ran into the same confusing rule in the book. He came home one night holding it up and said, "This makes no sense." And all I could do was smile.

It wouldn't be the last time I'd be accused of not following the rules. Ironically, the truth was the opposite. I cared so much about following them I tripped over myself trying.

Even after that embarrassing oopsie, at the end of the game, many parents came up to us and told us good game. After everyone had left, Laura and I looked at each other, questioning, "Are all the games going to be that easy? Are we doing that good of a job at our practices?"

"Can't be, right?" Laura asked.

We knew there was no way our little team of misfit beginners with four five-year-olds was that much better than the other teams. But the victory felt pretty good… until our Honda Pilot wouldn't start and Coach B was gracious enough to give us a jump. The coach we had just stomped in the game gave my family's car a jump to get home.

And that's when Coach Laura came up with another great idea for our next huddle: talking about the value of "good sportsmanship."

GAME TWO

Game two was my wake-up call: We couldn't just keep running the kids through the basics, we had to *actually* teach the game. We had drilled "run through first" so well in those first few practices that half the team thought the finish line *was* first base. Second? Third? Home? Anyone? Optional to these kids, apparently. By our third practice, performance was looking about the same as the first two. Which is to say… not nearly enough improvement was happening.

During the second game, we discovered the hard way that outs don't just happen at first, they happen everywhere. In tee ball, you become accustomed to the players only throwing to first base after every hit. And because we did so great on that first game, we didn't think to improve in that area. But, yes, outs happen at all bases in coach pitch.

And, oh, did they happen to us in our second game of the season.

We lost. Big. I can't remember the score (17-3 rings in my head), so let's just say we got humbled by the Yankees as badly as we had humbled the Cardinals the week before. We made no outs, couldn't hit, and our base running was… creative. Later, I'd learn their coach was about to move up to majors, which meant the Yankees had older kids and a coach with plenty of experience. Definitely more than us, anyway. None of that felt like an excuse, though. If anything, it lit a fire. I left determined to level up our practices, and teach the kids to get outs and "race to the base" like their lives depended on it.

I knew we weren't headed for a winning season. But I also knew what my own five-year-old was capable of. If he could do it, the others could, too. And if the five-year-olds could, then the six-year-olds had no excuse. I might not have the oldest or most seasoned team, but I was not about to sit back and accept losing every week.

That's when I started saying, "Race to the base." I'm sure the phrase existed somewhere in baseball before me, but I'd never heard it, and the kids instantly got it. Simple sayings stuck: "Race to the base." "Get mad at the ball when you swing." "See the ball, hit the ball." That was the language we learned to use with them.

Of course, some strategy had to wait. I could argue with my husband all day about teaching double plays or having outfielders back up bases. Sure, it's good baseball, but at six years old, half the time they're backing up the wrong base and the ball is just sitting in the grass. We had bigger battles to fight first.

CHAPTER 5

Losing Streak

This is painful to write. After that loss, we dropped three more in a row. Suddenly, we were 1-4. Ouch.

I don't like to lose. My husband doesn't like to lose. My brother-in-law, Ryan, *hates* to lose. And my sister, like me, hates letting people down. That part stung the most.

At one point in the season, both my nephew, naturally gifted at baseball, and my niece, athletic as they come, were on losing teams. Here were these hardworking kids, giving their best, and yet week after week, no wins. I couldn't shake the feeling that Ryan was stuck watching them pour their effort into a game that kept handing them disappointment and that I was part of the reason why.

From the moment you meet Ryan, there's a firmness about him that's impossible to miss. He's strong in his beliefs, black and white in how he sees things, and direct in how he says them. There's no guessing with Ryan. No decoding. You know where you stand, even when you don't love what he's telling you. Everyone could use a Ryan in their life, even when it's not a cakewalk.

He's had two professional jobs his entire adult life. That's it. He's consistent in a way that feels rare, grounded, and intentional.

He thrives on routine. He's painfully introverted, so I understand him in this way probably more than most people. Ryan doesn't shift his opinions easily, but when he does, it means something. His words carry weight because he doesn't hand them out casually.

That's why a recent group text between the four of us still makes me laugh. Aiden had been drafted into kid pitch majors, a different league than the Y and a real step up. Laura was nervous, because of course she was. Aiden was younger and smaller than all of the kids in the league. Phillip jumped in with his usual optimism, laying out all the positives, including how consistent pitching in majors versus the chaos of kid pitch minors would make it easier for him to hit. And then Ryan replied, "I agree with Phillip's optimism, too."

I sent a GIF of a man falling out of his office chair. I was stunned with that comment.

Optimism and Ryan don't usually coexist. Ryan agreeing with Phillip is even rarer.

Laura and Ryan are real-life Topanga and Cory, or Winnie and Kevin. If the Savage brothers (the actors played by Cory and Kevin) had a quieter, firmer brother who stood slightly off to the side but always had their back, that would be Ryan. He even looks like he could be one of their siblings. Same general build. Same presence. Just more reserved. More serious.

So when the losses started piling up that first season, Ryan's role mattered to me more than he might have realized. Let me be clear: Ryan wasn't blaming me. There were multiple times he would come up to me and tell me the parents supported me in whatever decision I made. When he thought I was making bad calls, he'd tell me straight to my face. He's more than a brother-in-law; he's practically my actual brother.

But none of that mattered in the moment. I took the blame. I was the coach.

No one in our family expected a championship season in our first season. But losing four games in a row hit me hard. I remember one drive home especially well. It was a bright, sunny day, the kind most of our games ended on, right around late morning or noon. We were about five minutes from our neighborhood, driving past a cemetery, when I couldn't fight back the insecurity any longer.

I found myself thinking about the first game. The "Good game, Coach" comments I loved. Craved, even. After four losses, parents were still kind and supportive, just quicker. Folding chairs. Loading kids. Heading out. I noticed my players' heads weren't held quite as high. The silence sat heavy with me.

Dylan was in the backseat, and I kept my voice low with my sunglasses on, so he wouldn't see or hear the tears creeping in. I whispered my doubts to Phillip as they came spilling out.

"Am I doing a terrible job? Maybe I'm not what these kids need. Maybe I made a mistake. Maybe I'm the worst coach." My voice quietly cracked.

"Crissy, no," Phillip said, steady and matter-of-fact. "Don't do that. You know you're doing great."

"I actually don't know," I said.

And then, to my surprise and mild horror, Phillip brought Dylan into it.

"Dylan," he asked, continuing to look ahead while driving, "do you like your mom being your coach?"

I wanted to stop him. My body clenched. I was obviously trying hard to hide this moment from Dylan. I never wanted him to think coaching him made me sad.

"I love it!" Dylan said immediately, enthusiastically, and with no hesitation.

Phillip nodded, still facing the road. "There you go."

I started to laugh through the tears. "OK, but see, I did need that."

It wasn't just about the scoreboard. The real fear creeping in was bigger: I wasn't strong enough to lead these kids. That instead of making an impact, I was failing them in a way that would stick. The emotions were a roller coaster, and I was hanging on by a thread.

STANDING MY GROUND

Losing is one thing. But what gnawed at me was the feeling I wasn't standing my ground.

If you've spent five minutes in youth sports, you know some coaches will bend the rules just to win. I still don't understand it. My high school friend once told me a piece of wisdom her parents gave her: "You can't expect everyone to react like you would. They aren't you, and they may not be as nice as you." That stuck with me. And, yet, instead of lowering my expectations, I just judge people harder when they don't act right. (Sarcasm, but also not.)

At the very least, volunteer coaches should play by the rules. But plenty of dads are trying to live out their dreams through little Johnny, with egos big enough to block the sun. For me, it wasn't about ego. What mattered more was raising kids who played with integrity. If we were going to win, it would be by playing fair.

The one big criticism about me from other teams and coaches was my pitching. Some parents and coaches said I pitched too close. Ryan also admitted it would raise his eyebrows if he was on an opposing team (I told you he was honest with me). I thought about my pitching more than I'd like to admit. But here's the truth: I couldn't consistently get the ball over the plate from the rubber. I didn't throw underhand because I was instructed not to (and, by the way, better off for it in the long run!) David made it clear: We could pitch from where we needed to. Some coaches were too proud to move up, or refused to kneel, so their kids didn't hit. **My players hit.**

I'd move closer for the five-year-olds, then step back a few feet for the older kids. Over time, I built strength, but I'd still adjust depending on the player. Pitching to young kids isn't about proving you've got a fast ball; it's about giving each batter a ball they can hit. If there's no hitting, there's no game. Hard stop. So if that gets me dragged in some Facebook mom group (you know about those moms groups on Facebook, y'all!), so be it. I don't see those parents out on the mound.

The real rule-bending that season wasn't pitching. It was positioning.

Some coaches were stacking the infield, cramming extra kids around the mound and between bases. Two, sometimes three players near the pitcher. An extra shortstop. Another kid drifting between first and second. Meanwhile, I was sticking to what felt like the spirit of the rules. Every kid plays. Extra players go to the outfield. This wasn't tee ball anymore. It was supposed to be baseball.

Watching other coaches try to win by stacking the infield was infuriating.

Then there was the overthrow rule.

If you're not familiar with youth baseball, here's the short version. When a ball is thrown past a base and gets away, some leagues allow the runner to advance one extra base. Some allow two. And some, especially with younger kids, don't allow any at all. The idea is similar to stealing. At certain ages, it's just too advanced. It stops being about learning the game and starts being about exploiting chaos.

In our league at the time, the rule allowed one extra base on an overthrow. The Giants' coach knew exactly how to use that. He ran his kids hard, counting on the fact that six-year-olds are still learning how to catch and throw. One overthrow turned into another, and suddenly his runner was rounding third on a soft infield hit while my kids stood there confused, wondering how things unraveled so fast.

It wasn't just aggressive. It was discouraging.

To protect our team, I started coaching the kids to get the ball back to the pitcher's mound as fast as possible so the play would stop. That meant no chance at an out, but at least it kept us from getting steamrolled. The downside was obvious. Instead of learning how to make plays, my kids were learning how to throw the ball directly back to the pitcher.

Eventually, the league threw out the overthrow rule entirely in coach pitch minors, and thank goodness. Some leagues need it. Some don't. For this age group, at the YMCA, removing it helped kids learn the actual fundamentals of baseball. Because when five- and six-year-olds are still figuring out which base is which, turning a missed catch into a home run doesn't teach them much of anything.

The rules weren't just confusing the kids. They were starting to test me, too.

A real turning point came in that same Giants game. One of my runners scored, and their coach argued him back to third. At the time, I let it go, thinking maybe he saw something I missed, still giving him the benefit of the doubt. Rookie mistake.

Next inning, I watched his runner take two bases on an overthrow.

If this were a movie, here's where the dramatic music would kick in. I took three giant steps toward the infield and shouted so I would be heard:

"NO, NO, NO! THAT RUNNER GOES BACK!"

I waved my arm, pointing to third base. "HE TOOK AN EXTRA BASE ON THE OVERTHROW!"

The ump agreed. The Giants' coach grumbled, shrugged with an eye roll, and sent the runner back every bit as begrudgingly as you'd expect.

And just like that, adrenaline surged. I had stood up for my team. For once, I wasn't the polite, second-guessing rookie coach. I was their coach.

For a second, doubt crept in. *Did I just look rude? Too aggressive?* But then I heard the parents cheering. My husband called out, "That's right, Coach! We're behind you!" and I knew I was right to make my voice heard.

This was the moment we all realized, me included, just how far some coaches would go to win, and how far I was willing to go to protect my kids.

That was the game I found my voice.

With getting our butts handed to us during that game, I didn't realize all the players he had on the infield. I'm sure I noticed how crowded it looked, but that was our third game, and I wasn't as observant as I should have been. My focus was on my players. I trusted that volunteer coaches for a CHILDREN'S game would do the right thing and have my same perspective. This game was a turning point for me.

The next game we lost yet again, this time to the Rangers. Turns out the Rangers' coach was a wolf in sheep's clothing himself. He was certainly bending a couple of the rules, but his team was so much stronger than ours, it didn't necessarily matter. He seemed nice enough. We were just the weaker team.

Within this timeframe, of us playing the Giants and the Rangers, we ran into Coach B. He pointed out how many players were at the pitcher's mound when he played the Giants. This conversation was another wake-up call for Laura and me. Turns out, the Rangers stacked the infield as well.

Our husbands started to observe more also. Phillip is even more outspoken than I am so he would start calling out unfair plays as he saw them. We had many conversations about the fine line between him calling out and getting carried away. He's loud, but not malicious. He sticks up for us. Sometimes he can even stick up for the other team *too much*. He used to be known for shouting out calls more favorable to the other team.

At the end of the day, Phillip's heart is in the right place. He wants fairness, he wants to see the kids shine. We're the opposite of the Rangers' and Giants' coaches; if there was a team quite a bit weaker than us, we made sure there was still a game. We cheered for the other team. We championed them when they made good hits—a good hit is a good hit on either side. We would shake up our positions to give the other team a shot at not getting out as often. But what my husband needed to learn in my first couple of seasons coaching was, when the game is competitive, **zip it.** Let the ump make the call. There's been a few times my husband made calls not in my team's favor. We laugh about it now, and, ultimately, he has helped us win overall through his teachings to me. But, whew, we had some heated discussions on car rides home at times.

Within the four-game losing streak, I learned a lot. Laura learned a lot. We all learned. We began to hate losing. Conversations about baseball consumed us. Laura and I talked about it every chance we got. We'd stay late after the games, watch other teams play to see how those games were handled. On Father's Day, we went out to brunch after the game and went over each player's actions, their behaviors (good or bad), and talked about our strategy for the next game based on what we'd learned. My dad and stepmom were fascinated and laughed at how the conversation kept shifting back to baseball.

Phillip was right: Coaching baseball became my Flesh and Blood card game. This was absolutely what I was supposed to be doing at this point in my life.

CHAPTER 6

Advocate For Yourself

At one of those games Laura and I stayed behind to watch, I got the best coaching tip I've ever received, and I'm still a little mad at myself for not seeing it sooner: Fun comes from confidence. And confidence comes from playing where you're good.

There we were, standing behind the fence at home plate, chatting with David while we watched. He pointed to the field and said casually, "You see that? You need your two best players at pitcher and first base. That makes all the difference."

Everything else faded out. I swear there was a lightbulb over my head that everyone could see. In that moment, it felt like permission, the kind you don't realize you're waiting for until someone hands it to you. Play your best players where they can shine. Of course!

Putting a kid at a "cool" position when they can't handle it isn't fun. Not for them. Not for the team. Not for the coach scrambling to clean it up afterward.

That's not to say players shouldn't be moved around. Of course they should. Sometimes a kid wants to try first base, and they deserve a chance. Sometimes you learn a lot by seeing what *doesn't* work. But it's also important to explain, in kid-friendly terms, why someone is batting where they are or playing a certain position, and how that spot plays to their strengths.

That feeling was familiar.

When I became a first-time people manager in my corporate job, delegating was one of the hardest shifts for me. I was used to being the one who just did the work. I remember thinking, *Why would my manager ask me to do something that would take them five minutes to handle themselves?* I didn't understand it until I learned, really learned, that delegation wasn't always about efficiency. It was about growth. Letting people operate in their strengths. Trusting them. Stepping back so they could step up.

Looking back, what's interesting is no parent ever said a word to us about positions in those early games. Not the parents of the stronger players. Not the ones who probably could have. No "Hey, you might want to try him here," or "You'll see more success if you move her there." Whether that was trust, restraint, or just kindness, I don't know. But they let us coach. And in a world where everyone has an opinion, well, I guess that was notable.

I was the coach. Of course I could put players where I knew they would be most successful. Of course I didn't need to worry about who thought what, or whether someone assumed favoritism. If the team improved, if the kids gained confidence, if we started winning because players were set up to succeed, the direction of the whole team would change.

And it did.

Part of what held me back early on was my relationship with the rulebook. There was language in there about rotating players, and I took it literally. Too literally. I didn't yet understand the difference between fairness on paper and fairness in practice. This was one of those lessons I had to live through to understand.

Now, I know not every league works this way. Some leagues require strict rotations. Kids can't play infield more than a certain number of innings, or they have to switch every inning. And while I've heard great things about leagues with those rules, I have a lot of empathy for the coaches navigating them. As someone who rotated constantly simply because I didn't know better at first, I know how hard that balance can be.

But in our league, at this level, the lesson was clear. Playing to strengths didn't just make us better. It made the game more fun.

For everyone.

And listen, I know people have strong opinions about this—social media is full of them. Here's mine: Yes, it's crazy when leagues or travel teams try to lock kids into one position for their entire career. BUT, within a single season? Kids need a chance to *master* a position or two. That doesn't mean Johnny can't move from outfield to first base the next year; it simply means he should get good where he is right now. Because that's when baseball is the most fun. It's the same reason my players love hitting, because they *hit*. They get on base, and then they succeed. And when kids succeed, they smile, they want to keep playing, and everybody has fun.

After four straight losses, it was time for us to have fun again. I was determined to turn the season around. We had eight games total, and at 1-4, I wanted to at least break even. I didn't want to be the one woman coach who came in dead last. More than that, I didn't want to let the kids down; they were trying hard, and the parents could see it. We practiced rain or shine. One evening, it rained, and six players stuck it out until it turned into a downpour.

I was so proud of them. It was messy, it was fun, and it showed me they were learning dedication.

And here's what I've learned: Learning to lose for kids is just as important as winning. If you never lose, you don't understand what it means to work hard for that win. If you never lose, you don't learn how to handle it when it happens. And when it eventually *does* happen, it won't be pretty.

When I first started coaching, I wasn't sure how much to emphasize winning. Should I share the score with the kids? Should I push them to get the W? Coming from tee ball, where scores do not matter at all, it felt strange to suddenly be rallying a team of little kids to "win the game." So, at first, I avoided scores altogether. But, of course, the kids started asking. They wanted to know the score. They wanted to know how they were doing. And of course they did, it's a game. A game they were working hard at in every practice.

Eventually, I started sharing the scores. When we lost, I'd tell them and use it as a teaching moment: "Here's what we'll work on next practice." When we won, we celebrated. Once, I promised them popsicles if they pulled out a victory. (Thank goodness they won that one!) I also started adding in extra practices because I learned other teams were doing it and we were allowed. I was nervous about asking too much; after all, the parents had only signed up for one practice a week, and I didn't want everyone to hate more practices.

But guess what? The parents leaned in. They wanted to win, too, and they wanted to win fairly. I bring this up because there's a common line in youth sports: "It's the parents and coaches who cause the drama and care too much about winning." And while there's truth to that (truth I have demonstrated already), here's the reality: The kids want to win, too. Above all, they want to play.

REDEMPTION

Game six had arrived, and I was relieved. I'm sorry to say it, but I was. I needed a break, and I needed a win. We were two games away from the season ending, and we were starting the team cycle over again, so we got to play the Cardinals.

God bless him, we love Coach B, but he wasn't able to squeeze much improvement out of his team, either. My team was itching for a win. I know he was, too, and we were his best shot. Whether or not he cared as much as I did, I'll never know. At least we both wanted to play fair. We respected each other because we were both new, both learning. That game started in a light rain; the Cardinals jumped ahead early, but we ended up pulling out the win. And when we huddled the kids afterward, we could finally say: "See? When you practice rain or shine, it pays off." That lesson stuck.

Then came the Yankees, the team that had started our losing streak. By now, our players had come a long way, especially at hitting. I also started putting them in smarter positions. Aiden and Oscar were both stepping up as strong players. I put them at pitcher and first base. The fact that they were friends was a bonus; they loved practicing together. Over and over: Aiden to Oscar, first to pitcher, pitcher to first. Reps, reps, reps.

Against the Cardinals, we'd managed a few outs, which gave the kids some confidence. Now, we just had to carry it into the Yankees game, and with any luck, build on it.

Before we started, we went over rules with the coach and the umpire: extra players in the outfield, the latest on overthrow calls, the usual. Quietly, I told myself not to expect too much. Sorry to my players if they ever read this one day, but Coach Crissy didn't always have faith. After multiple straight losses, I knew the gap between our rookie-heavy team and the more seasoned ones. I kept my hopes down to protect my heart, but make no mistake, I still wanted the win. Badly.

Another lesson you learn in youth baseball: Winning doesn't just depend on who shows up, but also on who does not show up. Parents of beginners, don't let this scare you off. If your kid loves the game, keep them in it. Put in the extra time: go to camps, take the extra practices, toss the ball in the backyard. I had to do it myself. I struck my own son out in both of our first two games, and it was brutal (underline, bold, all caps—**BRUTAL.**) Yes, he got some hits, too, but striking him out crushed me. So I hauled him into our small backyard and worked on hitting until he was smacking the ball so hard I thought he'd break the fence. From then on, strikeouts were rare.

All that to say, if there is a struggling player and he doesn't show up to a game… it helps the team perform better. I don't remember which kids missed this one, but by game seven, school was out, families were traveling, and a couple players had already decided baseball just wasn't for them. What we had left were families who were invested, dedicated, and having fun with us. And, honestly? Knowing how much my brother-in-law hates to lose, I was surprised, in the best way, by how many of my parents stuck it out.

By this point in the season, I was hobbling on a sprained ankle, on week two of the injury. Coach Laura, being a physical therapist, had armed me with a brace during the games and one of those ice-pack booties for after the games. A bum ankle wasn't about to keep me off the field.

I was also learning to raise my voice, literally. I was yelling more without embarrassment, which means I got hoarse quite a bit. I even squealed once or twice, which got a few laughs from the families in the stands. My job was to keep the kids focused and remind them where the play should be, and if that meant my voice cracking mid-call, then that's what it meant. I tried to ensure any presentations or important meetings I had at work fell on Tuesdays, knowing I'd need an extra cup of hot tea and honey on Mondays to repair.

And then it happened. During our breakthrough game against the Yankees, we were playing the best we'd ever played. So good, in fact, it rattled the other team. They did *not* like losing to our rookie Braves. One dad started heckling me from behind home plate, shouting that I was pitching too close. I let it slide for a couple of innings.

During one of the innings, we were at-bat and down to our last batter. Remember, in our league, if the fielding team doesn't get three outs, then the batters go through the whole line-up, and then they switch after the final batter hits.

Our batter hit, sprinted for first, and the pitcher fielded it clean to first. The ump called the runner safe. The coaches called the runner safe. The mom of the first baseman shouted, "The runner is out!"

A couple of parents near their dugout would not let the call go and started getting rowdy. The noise escalated quickly. I stepped in and calmly said the runner was safe.

That's when Laura caught my eye and quietly reminded me, "Cris, it doesn't matter, anyway. Last batter."

She was right. I exhaled and stepped back.

Moments later, the mom of the first baseman exploded. She charged at the ump and my base coach. The Yankees' coach finally told her the play didn't matter, anyway. It was time to switch innings.

Only later did I find out what I'd missed being heckled from the stands. That same mom said she hoped one of my best batters nailed me right in my sprained ankle. She wanted me physically hurt. Over a six-year-old's baseball game.

Evidently, it was quite tense over there, because when I got back to the pitcher's mound for our next at-bat, the heckling from that dad began again. Can you imagine? And eventually, I'd had enough of the heckling. I turned and firmly said loudly enough for him to hear, "I can pitch at this distance. **You** need to learn the rules."

That's when Rodney, Aaron's dad (also Laura's neighbor), spoke up beside me. "Coach, don't worry about that. Let me handle it. You focus on the game."

He was right. My job was to keep composure, to be the Christian example I wanted my players to see. Balancing grace and sticking up for my team and myself was tough. It was a balancing act for sure, one I didn't always get 100 percent right.

I had to advocate for myself. Sure, maybe I could've handled it differently—walked over, lowered my voice, explained politely. But you know what? He stopped after I said something. And, sometimes, standing up for yourself is messy. I am a sinner, I am not perfect. (Clearly!)

Looking back, it does make me chuckle, because it was wild. Truly, the absurdity of it all. Here I was, finally coaching **the** game of our season, and the opposing parents were losing it. In hindsight, I know tensions were higher that year because of the rule-bending from a couple of other coaches. This Yankees' coach wasn't guilty of it himself to my knowledge, but his parents had clearly been living in that storm and were quick to assume the worst. Still, that doesn't excuse it. No parent should be charging an umpire or shouting for a volunteer coach to get hurt.

After all that drama, the Braves took the W. Not just a win, but our first win against a non-rookie team. And we didn't just squeak by. We won by seven. The kids were beaming, the parents were cheering, our husbands were proud. It felt incredible. Maybe, just maybe, we were getting somewhere.

FINAL GAME OF SEASON ONE

Our last game was against the Giants again. We wanted to end our season 4-4. I wanted to break even. Coach Laura and I thought we had a real shot. Certainly, we wouldn't lose the way we had last time. We were going to make sure the rules were followed this time, and we had made some big improvements.

I planned to talk to the Giants' coach ahead of time about putting extra players in the outfield and playing the infield with proper positions. The Giants' coach resembled an older, taller, and bit thinner version of comedian Tom Segura. I can't unsee it now that I've seen it. For the sake of this conversation, let's call him "Coach Vince." I was extremely nervous. Laura gave me a pep talk ahead of time, and we discussed our strategy. "Do you want me to come with you? Or maybe not if he's not with his other coach, either." I agreed with the latter sentiment and decided to chat with Coach Vince on my own.

I took a deep breath and walked over to him.

The fields were wet, and the home plate had a pretty nasty mud puddle from rain from the day prior. My "in" to start the conversation on a positive note was approaching him about the field conditions and coming to an agreement on moving the plate up a couple steps so it could be on dryer land. Once we agreed on that, I discussed proper positions. It seemed to go fine; I was nervous for no reason.

Game time rolled around, and there was no umpire. My stomach sank. Against *this* team? We were the away team, so the Giants took the field first. After some back and forth, we decided to start, anyway. I reminded myself, *Grace, Crissy. Grace. Keep your tone calm if you need to address Coach Vince.*

At some point, David asked a mom from the Giants to ump. Not just any mom, the mom of the Giants' star player—their first baseman who never missed a catch. I'd even said once, "That kid cannot miss!"

And while she coached softball and knew the game, the rules weren't the same. I didn't realize how much that mattered until we got going. Still, in my mind, any parent should be able to ump fairly for YOUTH BASEBALL. For instance, if my husband had been asked, he would've gone out of his way to call against our team, just so no one could accuse him of bias. But, again, you cannot expect others to be wired the way you are.

Then it happened.

Taking the baseball mound, I looked around the field and saw it plain as day: at least two extra players in the infield. Coach Vince had nudged them back half a step so he could pretend they were "outfielders," but come on. He basically had a second shortstop between first and second, plus another camped between short and third. Not to mention the actual outfielders. He knew exactly what he was doing.

I stayed calm. I kept my reminder in my head: *Grace.* So I looked over and said politely, "Hey, Coach, can you get some outfielders, please?"

That's when he changed. His entire demeanor flipped like a switch. One second he was a regular guy, the next, something else entirely. His face twisted, his eyes went dark. (OK, maybe I've watched too many seasons of *Supernatural,* but I swear it was like demons took over his eyes.)

He started making a big show of it, sighing, grumbling, waving his arms like I'd asked for something outrageous. He boisterously ordered his kids to take a few steps back, then turned to me and sneered, "Is that far enough back for you, Coach?"

"Yes, that's better, thank you," I responded politely.

And it didn't stop there. He muttered under his breath the rest of the game, tossing little taunts my way. At one point, he dragged his sneaker in the dirt between second and third, carved a line in the infield, and told his player, "Here, stay behind this line. Coach wants you back here. Don't cross it." Then he looked at me and whined, "Is this good enough for you, Coach? Should he make sure he stands behind this line?"

I just stood on the mound, heart pounding, but kept my tone even and responded to his behavior. "Are you really acting like this? I just want our kids to play normal baseball positions."

Inside, though, I was rattled. Emotions were running high, and, honestly, the order of events are a bit of a blur. But I remember the feelings: tight chest, sweaty palms, that constant battle between keeping grace and wanting to scream.

We came out swinging, hitting strong in the first inning. SO strong! When the Giants got up to bat, their coach made sure to show us he didn't like it. He ran his kids, stretching every overthrow, pushing the limits of what the stand-in "ump" would call. One player managed to turn an infield hit into a run all the way from first to third; even when the pitcher had the ball, he kept the kids running. That was the moment I thought: *I should end this right now. Just pack it up, tell the Braves it's time to go party at the park, and save us all from this circus.* But I didn't. Because the kids deserved to play, even if the adults were losing their minds.

My husband, coaching third base, was sticking up for me, too, and pretty loudly. He hated seeing how lopsided the game was getting. At one point, he waved Aaron home on a risky play, trying to squeeze out something for the kids, and Aaron got tagged out. Right after, I told Phillip quietly: "We have to play *our* game." He nodded and agreed.

Still, the Giants' coach wasn't finished with me. He complained to the "ump" about how many adults I had helping on the field, as if suddenly, in game eight, this was a problem. In five seasons since, I've never once seen a coach pull that card. He only did it to silence Phillip, because Phillip was calling out where he was bending the rules with his runners. We let it go. Phillip stepped back. Let him have his tiny little victory. That was all he could come up with to try and throw the rulebook back in our faces.

And then came the moment I almost snapped. David was there by this point, watching from the sidelines. Another brutal call went against us, and I looked straight at him and said, "Really, David?" My voice wasn't angry, it was tired. Disbelieving. And I think David felt that, because he called time and brought me and the Giants' coach to the mound. David looked right at him and said, "This is about the kids. Think about how you're acting." Then looked over at me. I could feel my face burning. I was tempted, *so tempted*, to pull my kids off that field right then. Coach Vince said to me, "Oh, I remember what you did in our last game—you got rowdy."

My parents backed me. Ryan caught my eye and said, "Crissy, whatever you want to do, we are all with you." It was whatever I decided. But my adorable, big-eyed Braves were standing there, bats ready, waiting to hit. This was their last game. They deserved to finish, even if it wasn't fair.

Eventually, another "ump" showed up; he was actually a ref from flag football. (And yes, he brought *his own* rulebook. Suddenly, overthrows were two bases. At that point, we just laughed and rolled with it.) We lost, but we told our kids after the game that they'd played a great game and had definitely earned their party. Our kids walked into the end-of-season party with smiles and Ws in their eyes. They were ready to start thinking about playing another season. That was enough for me.

Later that very evening, at our neighborhood July 4th celebration, my niece, Riley, quietly told my sister a story. One of her friends, who happened to play for the Giants, had told her, "My coach said your aunt was sassin' him."

Riley, being Riley, brushed it off like a champ. She shrugged, changed the subject, and carried on. But I hated she had been put in that spot. What kind of grown man talks down about another adult to his young players, about a volunteer mom, no less? Bewildering doesn't even cover it.

And there I was, standing in the middle of a fun, bustling neighborhood event, feeling a mix of embarrassment, frustration, and doubt. Did I really want to go through that again next season? Could I put myself back in that position, facing the drama, the criticism, and the tension that came with it? Part of me wanted to walk away and let someone else take the reins. Everyone else, including our players' families and my son, were encouraging me to come back for one more season, but I wasn't sure I had it in me.

I never called the Giants' coach a cheater. I never poisoned my players against him. But I did pray. I asked God, "Why? Why am I being put through this for something so innocent as youth baseball? I didn't step up to coach for this. I thought I'd make friends, not enemies. I thought I'd be helping fill a need at the

Y, not dodging attacks from a man desperate for a win in coach pitch baseball."

But here's what I've come to see: The why isn't always about that one game. The why is bigger. Our kids—our world—need adults willing to fight for what's fair. They need to see that toughness comes from standing your ground, from holding people accountable, from pushing through even when the odds feel stacked, from refusing to let the wrong voices win.

And tough is exactly what my Braves became.

CHAPTER 7

Season Two

"It's a deal, Oscar," I said after two glasses of wine at our favorite hibachi restaurant.

Somewhere between the end of season one and the start of season two, we ran into Oscar and his amazing family at the hibachi restaurant. Everyone was thrilled to see each other. Oscar was coming back to play with us in the fall, despite the infamous Coach Tommy trying to recruit him. You know the type of coach: Parents either love him or hate him. Me? I'm somewhere in between.

My first real impression of Coach Tommy came when Oscar's mom approached me at a baseball camp. "Another coach is trying to recruit Oscar," she said.

Seriously? Recruiting seven-year-olds? Didn't he see I needed Oscar for *my* team? Let the kid stay put!

Suffice it to say, we were all relieved when Oscar chose to stay with us. He'd continue to shine, be a leader, and get to enjoy being one of the older players. Just like winning and losing, being the youngest or oldest on a team teaches lessons that stick.

At that hibachi meet-up, we chatted about the season ahead and whether Oscar was excited to play again. Oscar and I made a deal: If we did go undefeated, the end-of-season party for the players would be at that hibachi place, on us. The kids' eyes lit up like fireworks. I'll never forget how big Oscar's smile was when we shook hands on it. It became a running joke: "Really, Coach Crissy? Really pay for everyone if we go undefeated?" But the stakes were set, and Bradfords don't back out of their deals.

Of course, going undefeated meant overcoming the opponents who had haunted us last season. The Giants and the Rangers had merged into a "super team"; The Rangers: Season Two was going to be a grind. I had to ask myself honestly, did I really want to sign up for *that* again?

Then, enter Coach Preston. Dylan played on Coach Preston's tee ball team his first season at the Y. Palmer, Preston's son, and Dylan gravitated toward each other. They clicked immediately, and that connection stuck every season. They'd always say hi to each other. Preston and his wife, who was pregnant during that tee ball season, were always memorable to us moving forward. We have loved watching their kids grow.

When Coach Preston sat down next to me on a bench in the scorching South Carolina heat during a RiverDogs baseball camp, it felt like a reunion of sorts. I remembered him. He remembered me. And, yes, we both remembered the chaos of the Giants game from last season. His tee ball team was playing on the field over, and they overhead a lot of noise from our game. AKA—the Giants' coach yelling at me, and my husband yelling at the poor ump calls.

As we got to talking, I told him I couldn't believe how the Giants' coach had acted toward me.

"I could believe it," he said with a mouthful of dip, which was a common occurrence with Coach Preston.

I told him maybe I shouldn't have kept playing the game and we should have ended it.

He said, "I would have ended it." Then he added, "Absolutely, they are taking advantage of you because you are a woman."

It was the first time someone had said it out loud, without softening it, without pretending it wasn't happening.

"I am going to be bumping up Palmer to coach pitch in the fall, and if you want to assistant coach with me, putting our teams together, it would be great."

I paused, thoughtfully, and replied, "Thank you. I'm really going to think about that. That could be fun."

And that's when it hit me: I wasn't done. Not with the Braves. Not with Laura and me coaching side by side. Not with proving to myself I could keep doing this. In that moment, I knew I didn't want to be an assistant coach yet. I wanted to keep building what I had already started with our Braves. I wasn't giving up. It's not my style.

Coach Preston did end up waiting one more season to move up to coach pitch, anyway, and it all worked out. Phillip and Preston ended up coaching together in the same league for a year after I stopped coaching. On opposing teams, because it was more fun that way.

And now? Not only was I back to face the same intense coaches from last season, but I was also fighting to be $1,000 in the hole, determined to earn a hibachi dinner for the kids if we went undefeated.

For season two, we had seven players who stayed on our team—Dylan, Aiden, Oscar, Theo, Aaron, Samuel, and Connor—and we had several new players. At our first practice, you bet I watched them catch and throw and wonder what in the world I got myself into again.

What gave me the most hope, though, was watching the players who'd played with us the season before. They seemed worlds ahead of the players who had never played. That first practice of our second season was such an eye opener, looking at how fast these players learn. I knew if Coach Laura and I stuck to what we had learned from season one, we could get the new players caught up in no time.

The season was back in action, and our evenings and text threads were filled with who would play what position, the strategy for the next practice, and who needed to get more hitting in.

Season two was not without its bumps, though. Literally.

Coaching kids this young means injuries happen, and, for reasons I still do not fully understand, they seemed to happen mostly to my own kid.

The first one is burned into my memory. Dylan was racing one of his teammates toward the outfield when he tripped on the clay and face-planted hard into the dirt. When he looked up, his eye was surrounded by red strawberries and slightly bloody; it made my stomach drop, even though I knew it was only surface level. It could have been way worse. He was shaken, more surprised than hurt, and after a few tears and some reassurance, he was ready to keep going.

I still come across the photo of him on my phone in his bathroom that night with three skin-tone Band-Aids circling his eye, after we lathered the scratches in Aquaphor. He had the most annoyed look on his face, because he knew how awful he looked with the Band-Aids wrapped around his eye. That photo still makes me anxious. We got through it, however, didn't we?

And that's what most sports injuries are at this age, building a resilience in the kiddos they will need throughout life.

The others happened over time. During summer camp, Dylan wandered a little too close while Aiden was swinging and caught a bat to the forehead. It left a bruise and a small dent that stuck around for a few days. Another afternoon, a little sibling on the sidelines got stung by a hornet, sending all of us into action at once. Ice packs appeared, moms circled in, and calm eventually returned.

What stayed with me was how differently the kids and the adults experience it. The kids cried, recovered, and usually want to move on. As adults, as moms, we carry it longer. We replay it in our heads. We question ourselves. When a player got hurt, I felt the guilt of wondering if I should have prevented it, even when I knew I could not have.

After Dylan got hurt those times, and after watching how quickly other parents jumped in with whatever they had, I became *that* mom. Extra ice packs. Bandages. Wipes. Hydrocortisone. The packed-out first aid kit that lives in the trunk. The mack daddy of preparedness.

There is something important about letting kids keep going. Helping them shake it off. Not minimizing their pain, but also not letting it define the day.

That became my rule. If a kid got hurt and was able to continue, we ended on a positive note. Whether it was one good hit or a clean catch, if a player was struggling during reps, we made sure the last swing was a good one.

And somewhere in the middle of all that, we lost a game.

I think we won the first two, which gave me just enough false hope to think maybe we could go undefeated. We lost to the

Rangers. Then we beat the Rangers. We finished 6-2.

But season two wasn't defined by the record. It was defined by how much these kids were growing and how much they were still learning. Not just about baseball, but about listening, regulating emotions, and handling frustration. One of the biggest challenges that season had nothing to do with the scoreboard. It was learning how to coach behavior.

Most of our players were respectful and would listen when we needed them to. But that season, we had one player who struggled more than the others. He wasn't a good listener, he kicked dirt toward other kids, he tested every boundary we tried to set. If we told him to sit down and take a beat, he'd even test that. And then there were the harder days for all our players, when the otherwise great kids showed up distracted, frustrated, or just plain off.

At six and seven years old, you are not just coaching baseball. You are coaching emotions. Attention spans are short. Feelings are big. Some days, the ball is the least important thing happening on the field.

What surprised me most was how much the energy shifted depending on who was watching. When parents were present and engaged on the sidelines—not coaching, not yelling directions, just being there—the kids played stronger. They focused longer. They tried harder. I saw it over and over. I would strike one boy out every single at-bat during some games, then his dad would show up late from work and suddenly, WHAM. Double! All because Dad was there cheering him on.

It made me rethink a lot of what I thought I knew about the sidelines.

I have heard coaches say parents should stay quiet and let

kids listen only to the coach. And in some sports and at older ages, that makes sense. But at this level, with kids this young, sometimes they need a reminder that rules still apply. That effort is expected. Hearing it reinforced by a parent did not undermine us. It helped us.

You cannot expect six-year-olds to be locked in for an entire game. They are distracted by clouds, bugs, their shoelaces, and whatever snack they are hoping comes after. That is normal and age-appropriate.

One of the absolute highlights of season two had nothing to do with baseball at all.

It was the Dunk Your Coach fundraiser.

I hate the cold. It is one of the top reasons I live in South Carolina and not somewhere else. Season two was a fall season, and when the Dunk Your Coach fundraiser rolled around, the temperature dropped into the low fifties. For South Carolina in October, that is pretty rare.

The setup was simple. You buy tickets. You get a few throws. If you hit the target, your coach drops into a tank of cold water.

Naturally, my sister came prepared.

Laura had the foresight to bring extra cash so she could buy tickets for all of our players. Many of the kids bought their own, too. David's rule was three throws per ticket, which felt generous at the time and wildly excessive about my tenth dunk into the tank. Here is what I failed to account for: We had coached these kids really well. Like I said, they did win six out of eight games in season two! By the time the fundraiser rolled around, they could aim. I was dunked over and over again. The kids were shrieking with laughter. Parents were cheering. I was soaked, freezing, and trying to maintain my dignity while climbing out of the tank for what felt like the thirtieth time.

At some point, Laura walked up, completely unfazed, and said, "I have a change of clothes in the car. Want me to take over?"

"DO I EVER," I said, without hesitation.

I was proud of our team that day. Not just because they were deadly accurate, but because they showed up. We participated as a team, and we all supported the YMCA in a big way. As I've mentioned before, around 30 to 40 percent of the kids at our YMCA play sports on scholarship. Fundraisers like this matter. And our team leaned in.

After warming up and watching my big sister get dunked just as many times as I had, I loved taking it in and knowing this is what community looks like. Baseball brought us there, but moments like this were what made us stay together.

By the time we found our footing with behavior, something else had shifted, too. The kids were tougher. Laura and I were tougher. Losses didn't rattle us the same way, and wins didn't make us complacent.

I realized I wasn't just learning how to coach kids. I was learning how to manage chaos, make decisions under pressure, and stand my ground when it mattered. Those lessons didn't stay on the field. I carried them with me into my everyday life, into work, into situations where I needed to speak up instead of second-guessing myself.

And then David brought up the Y World Series.

The first season, we'd barely survived the schedule, the rules, and the learning curve. The team didn't find out about the tournament before it was too late. Vacations were already scheduled, and with that last game of season one, I believe most families were happy for a break.

This time, we were ready to give it a shot.

And, of course, the only team we'd be facing was the Super Rangers. Turns out, they were also the only other team able to get enough players to make it happen.

The Y World Series was coming.

And there was absolutely no way it was going to be easy.

CHAPTER 8

Dealing with Butthead Coaches (Never Giving Up)

Idon't remember every detail of playing the Rangers during the regular season in year two, and I think that's because David's son, Camden, was umping a lot of those games.

Cam was only nineteen at the time, but he was excellent. Confident. Clear. He didn't take any crap. He was fair and matter-of-fact. Honestly, it's no surprise he went on to become a United States Marine a year later. OORAH.

One of my favorite Cam moments had nothing to do with conflict. There was a game during season two that looked like it was going to get rained out. The forecast was dicey, and I was mentally preparing myself for the whole cancellation circus. Rescheduling. Text chains. The emotional buildup of game day, just to do it all over again. I hate that part.

Cam and team Braves both wanted to play, but there were coaches who did not.

David held off on canceling, like he often did, and sure enough, the storm moved right around us. The clouds broke, and the sun came out. It felt like we'd won something before the game even started.

As we were taking the field, Cam glanced over at me and said, "It's a beautiful day at Oakbrook YMCA. Let's play ball."

I laughed and said, "It's a beautiful day at Oakbrook!" I said this to him a couple times that day because it ended up a beautiful day. And because we didn't have to cancel.

That game ended up being a fun one. I don't remember who we played or what the score was, but I remember how relieved and happy it felt to play properly with an ump who followed the rules.

Cam also watched the Rangers closely. He'd seen them try to creep their outfielders up in other games, stacking the infield just enough to kill hits before they ever reached the grass. Laura and I had stayed to watch one of those games, and I remember whispering to her, "That ball wouldn't have been an out if that kid wasn't standing there in a made-up position."

So when it was our turn, I didn't have to raise my voice or make a scene. I'd subtly point it out to Cam, and he'd handle it. He'd instruct the player to move back to where they belonged.

Another small but memorable moment from season two was my ongoing experiment with kneeling to pitch. David encouraged it a lot. I tried in the first few games of the season. I bought knee pads, because pitching on my knees was wrecking them. But, eventually, I remembered something important: I'm only five feet tall!

Standing gave me more power and better control, which ultimately resulted in stronger hits for most of my hitters. So I stood back up. One day, after a big hit, I overheard Cam say to David, "See, she's standing to pitch."

That made me chuckle.

David was right about a lot in teaching and coaching baseball. Kneeling worked for many coaches. Just not this already-short-to-the-ground one.

While I don't remember every regular season game in season two, I remember the Y World Series Championship vividly.

A double header was decided with two games, back-to-back, something these young players were not yet used to. We told the boys to rest up (they were all boys that season). They showed up buzzing with energy. All in.

Cam was blue (the ump), thank goodness.

Before the first pitch, we had to establish, once again, that there would be no extra short stops between first and second base. Yes. This again.

The former Giants' coach (now Rangers' assistant coach—Coach Vince) didn't lose his mind like he had the season before, but it definitely ruffled his feathers. I think he held back because of the Rangers' head coach. And while the head coach was more level-headed, maybe more polished, he still wasn't a peach. As I told Laura, he's the one who chose to merge teams with that guy. So take that how you will.

Game one of the championship was, unfortunately, a master-class in how a batting line-up can undo you.

It didn't help that the former Giants' coach managed to get in my head again. He made yet another comment under his breath about me "following the rules." Apparently, nothing rattled this grown man more than a woman calmly insisting the game be played correctly. Strong, confident men who are totally secure with themselves always need to mutter about it, right? Feel free to imagine my eye roll here.

But the real damage was from my line-up.

I had Oscar toward the bottom of the line-up. As the clean-up hitter, of course! Except, **not** of course, because in youth base-ball, you want your stronger hitters earlier in the line-up so they get to bat more. We were hitting fine, but we weren't getting as many runs in as we could have. We left runs on the field, and the strikeouts piled up. Fielding mistakes crept back in at the worst possible time. In a weak moment, my brain turned on me.

This is karma, I thought. *I made them follow the rules like the goody two-shoes that I am, and now I've doomed my own team.* I felt responsible. Again.

When it ended, the boys held their heads high long enough to shake hands.

Then they reached the dugout, and three of my players immediately started crying. These were not kids who cried easily. Watching them fall apart undid me in a way I wasn't prepared for.

What did I get myself into? I thought. *God, please don't let me keep letting these boys down.*

The parents did what parents do best: They took them to lunch and reset them. I imagine there were some seriously good pep talks and maybe a few prayers of their own thrown in there.

The boys who came back for game two were different. They were our Braves. Smiling, tummies full, and all excited for the game ahead.

Oscar Sr. pulled me aside and helped me rethink the line-up. If they didn't get outs, our best hitters got to bat again in the same inning. So we started Oscar first, then stacked our strength behind him. Oscar. Aiden. Dylan. Connor.

It was simple and smart. It was exactly what we needed.

I shifted the field positioning, too, putting our strongest fielders where the ball had been finding gaps in game one.

And then we went out there, and those boys started hitting BOMBS. One after another. Loud contact. Hard runs. The momentum was building with every swing. I could feel it spreading through the dugout with the kids and into the parents in the stands. They fed off each other. Swing after swing. Run after run. You could feel the confidence spreading, inning by inning.

That was my and Laura's team. And the other team felt it. You could feel the shift when the game stopped going their way. The coaching got louder. At some point, our parents overheard one of their coaches telling his runner to shove Oscar as he ran to third.

And sure enough, one of their players did.

Cam saw it immediately and stepped in, telling their team to not allow that to happen again. The explanation came quickly from their side: Oscar was "standing in the baseline."

And even after this incident and the warning, when we were at-bat, a Rangers' player took his glove and whopped it on one of my player's helmets as he was safe running to second.

This was the first time I had seen it myself, but I had multiple parents tell me this wasn't the first time they saw this player putting their glove on our players. My first instinct was denial. Surely that wasn't intentional. Kids this age get distracted. They swing gloves. They miss cues. Most of the time, they genuinely loved seeing each other. They went to school together! They cheered for each other.

As my brain was still registering what I saw, the crowd went quiet, and J's dad, a large firefighter, shouted, "GET YOUR HANDS OFF MY SON!"

His mom chimed in, not as loudly but stern. "It's happened more than once—he needs to stop putting his hands on our players!"

A time-out ensued, Cam and the coach talked to the player, and, eventually, the game continued. It's my understanding it was getting ugly in the stands. What I remember was telling myself to carry the grace I'd wanted to have more of the season prior. To keep my cool—and besides, we were coming back! BIG TIME.

At one point, Phillip came back to the game after having to leave the tournament for a short time. I didn't even see him at first. I heard him. His Honda Accord is a hybrid, and it has this soft little hum to it. I always say it "sings" when it pulls up. Ryan heard it, too. Before Phillip could even open his door, Ryan waved him down and motioned for him to stay put. Don't get out. Don't say anything. Don't jinx it. We were making a grand comeback.

So Phillip did exactly that. He quietly stayed in the car. Watching from a distance. Fully participating by doing absolutely nothing.

And I loved that. I was relieved when I noticed Ryan telling Phillip to stay put. We were all in it together, just looking out for the game and the kids, everyone doing their part, even if that part meant sitting silently in a Honda and refusing to move.

And you guessed it. **We won!** I don't remember the exact score, but it was something like 38-26. The kind of comeback where you look around afterward like, *Did that just happen?*

I always joke that I don't know what kind of magical ice cream our parents must have given those boys during the lunch break, but, whatever it was, it worked.

But, honestly, it wasn't ice cream. And it wasn't luck. It was our families.

After that first game, we all knew what needed to happen. Those boys needed to be lifted back up. They needed to feel proud again. We hyped them up and reminded them who they were. When they came back onto that field, they came back together. And you could feel it. That was us at our best. A team in every sense of the word.

And that's what makes what happened next so frustrating. Because instead of this moment being remembered for the comeback, the grit, and the community behind those boys, it was once again overshadowed by the behavior coming from the other side of the field.

The parents of the boy who hit my player with the glove came over after the game ended. They apologized to me and to J's parents and told us they were just as confused as we were. They said their son had never acted like that before in a game, and they had him apologize, too.

I appreciated that more than I can say. I know it wasn't easy to walk over in the middle of all that tension, and they did it, anyway. They handled it the way you hope a parent would—with calm sincerity, focused on teaching their kid to do the right thing.

That apology only reinforced what our parents had been saying. They'd overheard things from the other side of the field that didn't sit right. Instructions that crossed a line. Still, we accepted the apology and moved forward.

J's parents came over next and apologized to *me* for yelling and for nearly stopping the game. I told them they had nothing to apologize for. They were protecting their son. I would have done the exact same thing for mine.

For a brief moment, it felt like the dust might settle. Like maybe that was the peak of it.

We were now tied 1-1 in the Y World Series Championship, which meant there was a third game on Monday evening to decide it all. David called both head coaches to the pitcher's mound. Laura stayed back near the dugout, close enough to see what was happening, close enough to step in if she needed to.

David and Cam made it clear the Giants' assistant coach was

not to approach the mound. He was told to stay in the dugout. He did not like that.

The Rangers' head coach started talking about how his parents weren't sure they wanted to play the third game. They were discussing forfeiting. David did what David does best: He circled around the conversation. He talked about the kids and how it was all for them. He tried to give perspective.

I listened, then calmly asked Coach, "Why wouldn't your parents want to play us?"

He shifted his weight and said, "Well… you know… a multitude of reasons."

I waited. I've learned listening and pausing in moments like these help me ensure I'm understanding the situation fully and not responding too quickly.

"But," he added, "we get a lot of comments about your pitching."

"OK," I said. "My pitching and… what else?"

Silence.

David stepped in. "She pitches to get the ball over the plate so the kids can hit, OK?" he said. "Why would that stop you from playing the game?"

The Rangers' coach muttered something that didn't answer the question. David and Cam chimed in about the Giants' coach's behavior, and the head coach said he understood his assistant coach had been doing too much. That he'd tried to calm him down. That he wasn't blaming me, exactly, but it seemed like his parents still wanted to forfeit. I mostly listened.

In the end, David suggested we all walk away for the night and decide the next day. So we parted with everything still unresolved.

I walked to my car where Laura was standing and told her the gist of the conversation. She said immediately, "They don't want to lose. That was an amazing game. They weren't expecting that comeback. Your pitching? That was insane. You don't for one second let them get to you, Crissy. Let's go eat dinner."

I got in my car and couldn't hold the tears back anymore. I was incredibly upset, and then immediately mad at myself for being upset. *How did I let another game get to this point?* I put my sunglasses on even though it was dusk. I didn't want Laura to see my tears as she got into her own car.

I replayed it all in my head. The only thing I'd pushed back on all series was positioning. That was it. I let Cam ump. I went with his calls even when I didn't love them (and there were some I didn't love). I followed the rules. We still got stomped in game one, and then we fought our way back and won big.

I hated my pitching in that moment. Even though I'd moved back toward the rubber as my arm got stronger. Even though I was standing now, pitching harder than I had all season. Even though my boys were hitting *hard.* They couldn't do that if I was just lobbing balls at them. I knew that.

But none of it mattered in that moment.

I felt disappointed, embarrassed, and angry. The boys had played their hearts out. They came back and WON. And, now, instead of getting their shot at a championship, I might have to explain to six- and seven-year-olds what a forfeit was. Sure, a forfeit was *technically* a win, but I wanted to finish the series the *right* way. I wanted to win because we won the game, not win because of a technicality. I felt defeated in the middle of a huge win.

Growing up, forfeiting wasn't an option. The only time we didn't play was if we didn't have enough kids. You sucked it up and finished the game or the series. That was how you learned resilience and developed character. I had a deep-seated stigma around forfeiting, and I couldn't shake it, especially in a children's game.

More thoughts flooded in. *Why would you teach kids not to finish? Why would that be the lesson? If anything, we were the ones getting knocked around out there. If someone should forfeit, shouldn't it be us?*

I didn't want anyone to think I didn't have my team's back. And, yet, forfeiting felt so foreign, so… not right. *Couldn't we just work this out like adults?*

Phillip and Ryan and the kids were waiting for us at the restaurant. When I walked in, the kids were already in the booth, smiling, loud, riding the high of the comeback. Phillip looked at me with an empathy he doesn't show easily. That's how I knew he understood.

"So," he said, "they want to forfeit?"

I nodded.

"They're scared to lose to you, Crissy," he said. "They're playing mind games."

Ryan chimed in. "They're scared to lose to you. One hundred percent."

"Yes," I said, "but that just seems so ridiculous to me."

Phillip didn't hesitate. "They're going to forfeit, And you're going to hold your head high and take the W."

Moments later, my phone buzzed. It was a text from David: *Rangers are going to forfeit.*

Laura and I decided we wouldn't tell the parents yet. We'd have the players show up in uniform. We wanted them to understand what it means to show up, to finish, to fight until the end, even when life doesn't go the way you expect. Instead, we'd turn it into a parents vs. players game. A game that was light and fun, and still honored their season.

Even with a plan in place, I couldn't stop replaying the days' events in my head. Sleep was scarce that night.

The next morning at 6:48, when it felt like I had just fallen asleep, Laura texted me.

"Try to think about something else today. Everyone is on your side and believes in you. We can't let that bad apple ruin everything."

For the rest of the day, I thought about what I would say to my players to make them proud of themselves. They thought they were showing up for game three. So did their parents. I tried not to spiral about whether anyone would feel inconvenienced by showing up for a game that wasn't going to happen.

Our players started to arrive, and it didn't take long for the parents to notice something was off. The other team wasn't there.

I lined the boys up along the fence behind home plate and asked the parents to stand behind them. David walked over carrying a box that looked suspiciously like it held trophies.

I crouched down in front of my sweet Braves, their faces lit up and curious.

"Hey, guys," I said, "what did you all do just now?"

They looked at each other.

"You showed up," I continued. "You put on your uniforms. You were ready to play. Yesterday in the first game, we didn't play our best, and we were pretty upset, right?"

A few heads nodded.

"But then what happened in the second game?"

"WE WON!" a few shouted.

"That's right," I said. "You showed up to play the second game. You didn't quit. And you played so hard that the team we beat decided not to come back tonight."

I took a breath.

"And because you never gave up, that makes you…"

A few of them squinted, thinking.

"The champions?" one said, hopeful.

"YES," I said. "The Braves are the Y World Series champions!"

The cheers exploded. Jumping. Yelling. Pure joy.

I went down the line, calling each boy by name and handing them their trophy. When I got to Dylan, the look on his little face stopped me in my tracks. That image of my son holding his trophy is one I'll carry forever.

The parents cheered, too, some still piecing together exactly what had happened but happy all the same. Gloves came out, laughter followed, and the parents vs. players game turned into the perfect ending and became a tradition.

In the seasons that followed, we stayed at the YMCA. We coached. We cheered on the sidelines. We watched new volunteers step in just as nervous and unsure as we once were, and without hesitation, we helped. We explained rules and offered grace. Gave them the benefit of the doubt people hadn't always afforded us.

Looking back, I still don't understand why some of the more experienced coaches chose pressure over patience, or power over community. But I do know this: That season shaped the kind of coach I became. And, maybe more importantly, the kind of coach I chose *not* to be.

CHAPTER 9

Season Three

The phrase, "A powerful lesson in never giving up," kept ringing in my head over the next few months. Because why in the world would I want to coach again after those two season endings?

We went for weeks not knowing Aiden would get one more season in this league. The cutoff was May 1, and his birthday is May 2. Oscar's birthday is May 8. All but two of my players could stay and wouldn't need to age up, and, of course, a couple of them wouldn't be able to return. If we coached again, we'd likely have seven or eight familiar faces; it was still *our* team, not a brand-new one.

I missed being on the sidelines cheering. I really did. During my husband's time coaching the minors, I became a full-fledged music mom. I played walkout songs for the players, cheered loudly, clapped too much, and loved every second of it. I enjoy watching and cheering as much as I do coaching.

The butthead coaches weren't returning. David's decision not to let the Giants' coach come to the mound during our final huddle in the championship cemented that. David had drawn a line, and maybe I was finally on the right side of it.

Oscar decided to try out a more competitive league, but his parents agreed to put him on our team, too, since there were only a few days of overlap. I felt like Oscar and Aiden could have an amazing season if we did it one more time. Our deal still stood: An undefeated season equaled an end-of-season hibachi party. The stakes were set, once again.

I wanted to pitch a home run to one of these kids to prove my meatball pitches weren't so terrible after all. Or maybe I'm a glutton for punishment. You can decide, since I'm learning not to care what other people think, anyway.

This time, we even had a sponsor, which was Oscar Sr.'s contracting company, and David really upped his game with the uniforms. The T-shirts were much more comfortable. (Hey David! Laura and I are *still* bitter you never put "COACH" on the back of the coaches jerseys. We earned that title, dang it!) David said he didn't think it wasn't necessary, and it wasn't a battle we chose to fight.

This season felt like a clean slate, and, honestly, that made me both hopeful and cautious.

Preston's Pirates were moving up from tee ball after staying in an extra season, which made me a little nervous. If he'd kept them back on purpose, he probably knew exactly what he was doing to get them ready… so I thought.

The Cubs' coach was a nice man, and his team had already been together for two seasons, which usually shows up on the field.

The new Rangers' coach seemed organized and confident, so I did not know what to expect from them yet.

The Seahawks were coming back for spring like always, but they'd skipped fall, so they felt like a bit of a question mark.

All of this mattered because season three felt different to

me. I wasn't wandering into it anymore. I wasn't guessing. I was planning. I was looking at coaches, rosters, and matchups the way someone who had been in the arena does. I knew enough to understand what we were up against, and enough to believe maybe, just maybe, we could rise to it.

That hibachi deal with Oscar was not in the back of my mind. It was right there in the front, waving at me every time I thought about the season. I wanted to go undefeated, not just because it would be fun, but because I wanted those boys to experience what it feels like to work toward something big and get there together. After everything we had been through, I felt like they deserved that.

I also wanted it for myself. I wanted to see what our team could look like when everything came together, when I applied what I had learned, and when our kids played with confidence instead of survival. I wanted to know if all that growing, all that stress, and all that effort had turned into something.

Of course, I was fully aware of the irony. I was strategizing this hard so that, in a few months, I could happily spend a very large sum of money feeding an entire team of children hibachi. But if that was the price of confidence, teamwork, a little redemption, and a lasting memory for these kids, I was more than willing to pay it.

My pitching was getting faster and more controlled, and I could adjust it depending on the player. I practiced a lot with Dylan and Aiden, moving around, trying slower, trying faster. Aiden liked a pitch right down the middle. One time, we timed it so perfectly he hit a home run during practice. Dylan was hitting triples like a champ.

I could feel myself getting better, and that changed how I carried myself on the mound.

I had a girl on my team again (Coach B's daughter), and I adored her immediately. Long blonde hair, skinny as a rail, and a serious expression most of the time.

One day, half joking, I asked her mom in front of her, "What does it take to get her to smile?"

Her mom just laughed. "Your guess is as good as mine."

A few minutes later, she stepped up to bat. I pitched it perfectly down the middle, and she ripped it straight back at me. My usual cat-like reflexes kicked in, but I was not fast enough. The ball smacked me right on the thigh.

She burst out laughing.

"Oh, OK," I said, rubbing my leg. "Now I know what makes you smile!"

I was taking my fair share of beatings in my third season. The players were getting stronger and hitting harder. I remember one practice where I walked away with three welts on my thighs because one of my boys was finally learning to drive the ball right back up the middle.

I never wanted my players to feel bad and change up their swings or get scared to hit it so hard, so I would just smile, laugh it off, and tell them they did exactly what they were supposed to do. Even though I got made fun of for my pitching throughout my time coaching, I loved pitching and watching the kids become increasingly proud. I loved finding their sweet spots.

Historically, I was impressed with my ability to get out of the way from a hit back to me. I never wanted the ball to hit me because then it would be deemed a dead ball—hits are precious in coach pitch, and I didn't want to risk redoing it.

Some of the other coaches look like an elephant in slow motion trying to get out of the way of the ball. I want to shout, "Move,

Coach, get out of the way. These kids have bases to run."

As the season began, we kept a close eye on our competition. Laura and I checked the app constantly, watching which teams played each other and what the scores looked like. Even so, I never let myself get too comfortable. After the last two seasons, I knew how quickly a game could turn on you. If two of my strongest players were out, I suddenly had a completely different team. If one big hitter had an off day and the other team showed up at full strength, we could still lose.

Still, the energy of this third season felt different.

Coaches were kinder to one another. My parents trusted me more. I understood what made a strong line-up. I felt confident putting players in their regular positions instead of constantly shuffling them around. I knew what to say that would actually resonate with the kids. Most of all, I knew reps in practice were our real path toward the undefeated season we were chasing.

The rules were clearer now, too. David, the coaches, and the umpires were mostly aligned, which took a weight off my shoulders.

We kept our rhythm of one regular practice each week and one bonus practice. One afternoon, I arrived a full hour early to a bonus practice, just to warm up my arm. Theo's mom happened to be driving by, and she rolled down her window as she passed the field.

"Love your dedication, Coach!" she called out. "Look at you out here putting in the hard work!"

"I have to!" I shouted back with a laugh. "I need to make sure I can actually pitch to these kids this season."

She grinned. "Your pitching is great, Coach."

We both smiled, and I went right back to tossing pitches to Dylan in the quiet afternoon heat.

Phillip, meanwhile, had started bringing his portable blower to every game to clear out the dugouts before the players sat down. At first, I thought it was pure overkill, classic Phillip.

But after one game where he forgot it and a couple of younger siblings got stung by hornets, I stopped teasing him about it. That blower earned its place in our baseball routine.

Our early schedule threw us right into the fire. We opened with the Pirates, the Cubs, the Orioles, and the Rangers. I swear David was trying to give me a heart attack. The Cubs were a returning team with a returning coach, already familiar with one another. The new Rangers looked just as strong, maybe even stronger, than the original Rangers from the previous seasons.

Phillip tried to calm me before every game. "You're going to win, Crissy," he'd say. "Don't worry."

Don't mistake my desire to not get complacent and be caught off guard for insecurity. The players were more confident as well. Most of them were older now, and they were better listeners, understood the directions, and could apply them.

The first game of the season had arrived, versus the Pirates. Once again, Phillip reassured me we would win. "Preston's kids are small," he said. "They aren't hitting yet." His comments didn't give me additional assurance. Coach Preston knew what he was doing coaching his players, and they put in the extra practices, too.

When game day came around, sure, we dominated them 35-1. There wasn't a mercy rule in our league. And even if there was, Coach Preston wanted to let the kids play as much as we did, so we kept playing the game. We shuffled our players around a few innings like we had the other seasons, but Phillip was right: Preston's kids were little.

I knew it had to be painful for him. I didn't take any real pleasure in that part of it. I've been on that side of the scoreboard, and I know how long those innings can feel. It never even crossed my mind to be petty and think, *Be your assistant coach now, bro.* OK, maybe it crossed my mind for half a second. I hope Preston laughs when he reads that.

Jokes aside, I felt the shift in the Pirates' parents immediately, the way they leaned forward on their folding chairs, the way the chatter quieted, that realization creeping in that says, *This isn't tee ball anymore.* Three seasons earlier, that was me.

Since there were seven teams that season, we played the Pirates again a few weeks later. That time the score was 20-7. Not a blowout, but a real game. Preston's kids had clearly found their bats.

It was another reminder of what I'd learned the hard way. At this age, kids change fast—week to week, sometimes even game to game.

One afternoon, I arrived early to our game, as I usually did, and the Pirates were still on the field playing. I found myself standing on the sidelines chatting with Preston's wife when another Pirates' mama, Donna, walked up to us.

"Your pitching is so good," she said. "I love watching you pitch. I can tell you know exactly where to pitch to your players."

I liked her immediately. She had no idea how much those words meant to me. I thanked her, and then, almost without thinking, I added, "Your team looks just like we did my first season." Maybe not exactly. (For the record, my Braves never lost by thirty-four points.) But they looked young, green, and full of potential. "They're going to improve so much, you'll see. They may look small at the plate now, but they'll grow fast."

Donna smiled, though a little uncertain. "OK. I hope so."

A year later, that conversation came back to me, in the best way.

Donna and I ran into each other at an off-season practice Preston was hosting for any kids who wanted extra reps. Anyone could show up. As soon as she saw me, Donna said, "Do you remember what you told me that day? You were right. They have gotten so much better."

I loved hearing that because it meant her kids had grown, gained confidence, and stuck with it.

Then, one year later, during my husband's final season coaching minors, Donna found me again, grinning from ear to ear. "We finally did it," she said. "It took us three seasons, but our Pirates finally beat the Braves."

I laughed out loud. I loved that moment. One of the boys whose mom I'd grown close to, Christie, had a son, Christian, who hit the game-winning run against Phillip's Braves. We'd seen these kids at camps, off-season practices, and pickup games. By then, it hardly mattered what jersey they wore. If we knew their name, Phillip and I were cheering for them. That's the kind of community we built at the Y.

Two more games had passed in season three, and our Braves were sitting at 3-0. We'd taken down the Orioles, and then came the Cubs.

This was the game where Aiden caught that pop-up at the pitcher's mound and fired it to first for the game-winning double play. I can still see it in my head: the ball hanging in the air, Aiden settling under it, the catch, the throw, the out. Our dugout erupted. We weren't cheering because we wanted to crush the Cubs. We were cheering because of what that play represented for us. Aiden had been practicing those pop-ups over and over, and, in that moment, all that work paid off.

Right after that game against the Cubs, I headed to New Orleans for a work trip. Waiting for us when I returned was the next big test of our season. I landed, unpacked, and almost immediately had to shift my brain back to baseball.

Based on our game app, we could tell the new Rangers team was good; they were 3-0, just like us. We stuck around and watched their games a couple of times, and it only confirmed what we already suspected. They could hit. They could field. Their coach pitched well, confidently, like a coach who had done this before. I could tell this was not his first rodeo.

We were coming off a team outing to the Charleston RiverDogs, our local minor league team. It had been such a great bonding night. Even our quietest players were laughing, joking, and acting like a real team. I felt hopeful walking into this game. Confident, but not naïve.

And then the Rangers gave us not a smidge less than *everything* we could handle.

From the first pitch, it was a battle. Back and forth. No shuffling positions this time. Every kid had to be locked in, exactly where they belonged. There could be no strikeouts, no lapses, no "learning moments." This was real baseball.

With two outs and a half inning left, the score was tied 14-14.

Dylan was on third, heading home for what would have been the go-ahead run. I can still see it in slow motion. The catcher planted himself at the plate, glove up, ready to make the play. Dylan, running full speed, slid naturally around him.

My heart dropped.

Sliding isn't allowed in our league. David had told us if it happened by accident, it wasn't automatic doom. The rule was one warning, then an out if it happened again. We'd never coached our kids to slide. Dylan just reacted like any six-year-old would in that moment.

The Rangers' coach insisted that in another game, the ump had called an out for one of his runner's sliding. Our ump said he had never called an out for sliding, but the Rangers were adamant. After a tense pause, we took the out.

In that moment, my stomach dropped. *Did I just lose this game for us?* I was panicked, trying to talk myself through it. It felt like the right call to accept it because the Rangers said it had happened to them before, and fair is fair, right?

"It's OK, Braves," I told them. "Shake it off. Let's go out there and get some outs so we can win this thing."

When a frustrating call happened, we aimed to teach them you don't sulk, you don't get upset in the dugout, you turn that energy into making great plays.

"Three up, three down!" I cheered them on.

I like to say they redeemed Dylan that inning. Because three up, three down is exactly what they did. They showed no mercy!

When we came back to bat, we scored the winning run. 15-14.

The Rangers even let us finish the inning so the kids could keep playing, and I will give them credit for that.

The second the game ended, I sprinted to Laura and hugged her. We jumped in circles like absolute lunatics. I did not care who was watching. We were halfway to hibachi, and we had just cleared one of the biggest hurdles of the season, especially after taking that sliding out.

Mid-season celebrating ensued, and I floated through the rest of that day on pure adrenaline. I was so elated, we did something we almost never do: Our family went out to eat **twice**, which is quite excessive, even for us.

We started with lunch at our favorite BBQ spot, then headed to Riley's volleyball game. After that, all eight of us ended up back at our house, where the kids tore through the backyard and the adults lingered on the patio with a few beverages. The afternoon had that easy, sun-soaked feel where nobody wanted the day to end.

Laura and I could not stop smiling. We talked nonsense, laughed too loud, and snapped what is now one of my favorite photos of us from that season. Somewhere in there, we tipsy-texted our girlfriends and families that we were still undefeated: "4-0!!"

At one point, Laura told me the YMCA had approached her about doing an interview. She wasn't entirely sure what it was for, only that it had something to do with her volunteering and our family's experience. Turns out, that interview was ultimately because her family was named our local YMCA "Family of the Year." I was genuinely thrilled for her. If anyone deserved that spotlight, it was Laura. She had poured so much time and energy into fundraising for the Y, far more than I could ever fully capture in this book.

I also, half joking and half serious, blurted out that maybe I would write a book about all of this one day.

Eventually, we decided it was time to fill our bellies again and headed to my first visit at what would become our favorite sushi spot. I had a glass of wine, as if I needed another one at that point. Luckily, Phillip was the designated driver. Dinner was loud, chaotic in the best way, and full of that exhausted, happy energy that only comes after a big win.

We all piled into one car to go home, and Laura captured the moment on video from the backseat of the Pilot. You have to picture it: Laura is squeezed in next to Riley and Dylan, both of them giggling and dancing until it dissolves into an impromptu arm-wrestling match. Aiden and Amelia are in the middle row with Ryan dramatically tickling them while "Under the Sea" blares from the speakers. I'm up front in shotgun, dancing and singing like I'm in my own personal music video, still proudly wearing my Braves jersey, while Phillip glances back every few seconds, grinning at all of us like his heart might burst.

What a win to pull through.

We ended up winning our next three games. One of them, as you already know, was against the Pirates, and the other two were against newer teams still finding their footing. By that point in the season, it felt like our Braves were finally hitting their stride.

And, yes, I did get my selfish little dream. Oscar hit a home run off my pitching. Actually, not just one. He hit two.

Coach Laura finally got to do what she had been waiting all season to do. She rallied the boys from the dugout, had them line up along the baseline, and led them in cheering as Oscar rounded the bases. The kids were completely lit up, jumping, clapping, shouting his name, practically spilling onto the field in pure joy.

And then, of course, we could not get them off the field.

They swarmed him, laughing, patting his helmet, huddling around him like he had just won the World Series. Oscar already had that bright, easy smile, but in that moment, surrounded by his teammates, it felt like it doubled in size.

All of that momentum, all of that joy, carried us straight into the final game of the season.

The final game of the regular season arrived on June 22, 2024, against the Seahawks. I had already told our parents I'd made reservations at the local hibachi restaurant. If we pulled out this win, the Braves were getting their celebration. By every stat and every bit of momentum we had built, we should win.

Our history with the Seahawks' coach was complicated. The YMCA partners with their school, so their roster was made up of players from their school community. We had friends of friends there, acquaintances, and generally positive experiences with most of the families. During the previous season's Majors Championship Tournament, their head coach had seemed to genuinely like us. We had cheered for his team against Coach Tommy's Angels (the infamously intense coach everyone in town knows, because we were rooting for the underdogs), and that clearly meant something to him.

At the same time, the Seahawks' coach could get prickly when calls didn't go his way. Competitive, sure, but sometimes a little sharp. So even though this *should* have been a straightforward game, I still felt a low hum of nerves.

We arrived, set up, and immediately noticed the weather was questionable. Over the seasons, we had learned that waiting fifteen minutes often saved everyone a reschedule. We had played in drizzle before, delayed games before, and been glad we waited it out. So when the radar showed the shower moving through, my instinct was to give it a moment.

I had talked to Laura, Ryan, and Phillip about how to play this out, and everyone agreed the weather looked like it was going to clear up and we should play ball. Most of the parents we side-barred agreed with keeping it on, too. Coach Laura agreed I should be upfront with the Seahawks' coach. Telling him about the party couldn't hurt; surely he would understand.

I could tell right away the Seahawks' coach was hesitant. He made it clear he wasn't thrilled about playing in the rain. I tried to be straightforward and respectful.

"Coach, we have our end-of-season party after this, and I'd love it if we could try to make this work. If there's no thunder or lightning, we'd love to let the kids play."

He said he wasn't sure his parents would be on board, but if the umpire said we could play, then they would.

We got through the first full inning, and it was 7-1 in our favor.

Then the rain really started coming down. Still no thunder, no lightning, but a steady, soaking rain. Everyone was checking their weather apps, and every one of them showed the same thing: This band of rain would pass. The sun was right behind it.

The umpire called a fifteen-minute weather delay. During that delay, I watched the Seahawks' coach pacing behind the fence, arms crossed, jaw tight, clearly irritated. I avoided eye contact and focused on keeping our kids calm, dry, and ready to go back out. Finally, he came over.

"My parents want to wrap it," he said.

I answered as evenly as I could. "Are you sure you can't wait just a few more minutes? We'd love to avoid rescheduling."

For a split second, the thought flashed through my mind: *Not another season ending like this.* Then he stopped, looked straight at me with sharp eyes, and said, "I don't care about your end-of-season party. That is not what's important here. The safety of these players is most important."

I felt my stomach drop. For a moment, I just stared at him. Not angry, not defensive, just unsettled. I wondered if he was seeing dangers I wasn't. Was I missing something? Was I too focused on finishing what we'd started? Was he implying I didn't care about the kids' safety?

I immediately reminded myself how deeply I cared about the kids' safety. We had delayed games before, which meant pulling kids away from any wet spots. We had waited out storms. I also believe that some rain, handled carefully, didn't have to end our season.

I simply responded, "OK, Coach."

I turned to Laura and Phillip for an update. "So… I think we just won 7-1."

They both laughed softly, not at him, but at the situation. Phillip immediately said, "Get the parents out there. Kids vs. parents."

We grabbed gloves, and as the rain began to slow, we took the field. The kids were laughing, parents were warming up their hitting, and, for a moment, the tension melted into pure fun.

Meanwhile, the Seahawks' families began packing up. Not all of them, but most. The sky shifted as the rain eased up. The sun came out in full force, and the field started drying right before our eyes.

Across the fence, the Seahawks' coach stood with his hands on his hips, watching us play, the sun now shining down on the diamond.

That's when we realized why he hadn't left. His car had a flat tire, and he ended up having plenty of time to wait after all. I've thought about that moment more than once. The symbolism isn't lost on me.

There's not a doubt in my mind that if the game had continued, we would have kept piling on the runs. Either way, the result was the same.

We'd won.

We were undefeated.

And we were about to show our players what hard work, resilience, and never giving up looked like.

Coach Pitch Minors Braves Undefeated Team, June 2024

Undefeated?

Undefeated. *Undefeated.*

Growing up, how many of us can say we had an undefeated season in sports? I couldn't say it. I was close in softball one season, but we ended up losing two games.

Every one of our players in season three worked hard at contributing to our wins. It was not simply luck and two crazy-pants mom coaches with something to prove.

Whether it was Aiden out there again and again, working on catching pop-ups until it finally clicked, or Oscar rushing over from his other league and going straight from one game into another without missing a beat, or my only girl in season three, who went through a stretch where she couldn't make contact for a couple of games, only to come back and say in her own words, "I got my hitting back," none of that happened by accident. It came from repetition, from showing up, from putting in the work long before the results ever showed up on the field. I felt confident we'd taught our little players to work toward a goal. Not only that, but I had also worked toward a goal. I didn't give up, even though at times, boy, did I want to. And, now, it was time to celebrate over a hibachi dinner!

I went around the table and asked each player what their favorite memory was of our season. I told them I had a lot to choose from but I was most proud when they were cheering each other on, during Oscar's home runs, or when they cheered on Aiden for his double play to end and ultimately win the game.

While we all got together to celebrate at hibachi, in true Coach Crissy fashion, the season wasn't quite over yet. We decided to enter the YMCA World Series Championship again. While I joke about being a glutton for punishment, the way I look at it is this—when my kids are learning something new, if a negative experience happens in that moment of practice, I try to end on a positive note. When Dylan got hurt and was bleeding out of his face from tripping on the baseball field, I still had him hit one more round to end on a positive note. When we would go through a bucket of pitches, twenty of them could have been solid hits and an overall great session, but if that last one was no good, I'd pitch until one was hit to the outfield. I was hopeful that by doing this championship, it would end my entire coaching experience on a positive note. Maybe, for once, our last game would be a full ending. A final full game.

Seven of our original Braves players were in for the championship, and three players got bumped up from tee ball to play with us. Sure, that had me a bit nervous that potentially these three tee ballers could lose our undefeated title outside the regular season, but the other teams also took tee ballers. I liked a good challenge, anyway.

Also in true Coach Crissy fashion, I was *nervous*. This time, however, more excitement was mixed in. Oscar could not play with us, so Aaron would step up as first baseman. A new-ish first baseman and three tee ballers. I thought I still had a good chance at losing. I didn't know the kids who were bumping up; it was anyone's game.

Unlike the previous season, there were four teams: Pirates/Diamondbacks, Phillies/Orioles, Seahawks, and us. David was doing what he had to do to let these players keep playing!

First game, full circle moment, we knocked out the Seahawks 28-10. Full confirmation we would have indeed beat them had that final game not gotten rained out. That felt great! Especially as the sweet tee ballers became a part of our team that game. During this first game, boy, was I nervous pitching to tee ballers. My mind wandered with questions. *Can they hit? Are their parents pitching to them at home?*

Miles, a little spunky kid with dark hair and a big smile, got up to bat, fouled one, then striked another. He said to me in the most chipper voice you can imagine: "Pitch it to me right here, Coach!" while gesturing his arms down the middle across his belly.

"OK!" I said. So I pitched it to him right down the middle.

BAM. This little four-year-old hit the ball out toward second base and ran down that first base line faster than a hyena. I sent a big smile his way as he stood on first base. When we locked eyes, he said, "Told ya, Coach!"

"You knew it, buddy! Way to go!" I responded.

Come onnnn! Can you get any cuter than that? At one point, he was doing something else adorable, and I looked over at his mom, and I said, "He is the best." She responded in her Southern accent, "He is definitely a trip."

Last and final game of the championship: Braves vs. Pirates/Diamondbacks. Our old buddies the Pirates. They'd gained a home run hitter from the Diamondbacks team, and they gave us a legit run for our money. Aaron stepped up at first base that game, and he certainly made an impression on the other team. Whenever he came out to play after this game, any coach around him would say, "Aaron's at bat, he's a ball player, everyone move back!" While we didn't get any home runs during the championship, our players were slamming those balls in the outfield! I was pitching farther back than I ever had before and was still nervous I was going to get my teeth knocked out.

Final score: Braves 18, Pirates/Diamondbacks 15.

After the game, Palmer and Dylan were chatting with each other and playing around like they do, and Dylan said, "Hey, Palmer, want to hold the trophy and take a picture with me?" He turned to me and said, "Mom, take a picture of us!"

Cue the proud mama moment. The kids on both teams were great sports in our last game. It's funny—reflecting on that last game is what launched what was to come.

Coach Preston became key in our ongoing YMCA baseball journey. Miles' dad, Coach Spencer, took over the Braves for a season to keep the kids together, and we love their family. Jonathan, the other tee baller, stayed with the Braves for three more seasons, and his dad helped coach. Phillip—Coach Phil—took over for two seasons because Coach Spencer needed a break for his job. And we all lived happily ever after. HAHA.

After that championship, though, the drama faded for the Braves, even though there was still some discourse with other coaches within the league throughout the seasons.

I settled into my new, very beloved role of music mom and coach's wife. And as skeptical as I was about the music for such an informal league like the YMCA, I *highly* recommend downloading the app, getting an inexpensive but high-quality bluetooth speaker, and playing some good ol' family sports music at these games, complete with walkout songs for the kids.

As I'm writing this, we just wrapped Phillip's second season of coaching the Braves' minor's coach pitch. It was Dylan's last season in this league. And I'm not too prideful to say I get teary-eyed when thinking about it, let alone writing about it.

This is what God had in mind for me and my little family.

I've since found out my husband is a phenomenal baseball coach. Without a doubt a better coach than me. His crazy antics are loved by all, and not only did he not lose any players to other teams like I did, but he also had parents request to be on our team. But I will never give up the chance to throw a small jab (I was, after all, the only undefeated Braves' coach).

All joking aside, Coach Phil is extroverted, loud, detail-oriented (he labeled magnets for his weekly line-up for Pete's sake!), and, somehow, got these kids hitting like they were all playing for the major league. He is an excellent pitcher (when he isn't trying to pitch fast balls to them to see how they handle it), and I loved watching him help the other teams when their players needed it. He offered to let two of our players play on another team so the opposing team wouldn't have to forfeit. He made sure a player, not a coach, said a prayer before every one of his games. He would fix the opposing batter's swing so they could get a hit in.

We built so many friendships and made so many wonderful memories. I'm so glad I convinced him to coach. Because it did take convincing.

Now, as we look to the future and decide where Dylan will play next since he has to bump up an age group, and decide tee ball vs. coach pitch for our youngest, we have a lot of uncertainty about the best path for our kids' journeys with sports. However, what we know for sure is our time volunteering is not over.

If you take any action upon reading this book, please inspire yourself, or someone you know, to volunteer. I think I've showcased well enough that you don't have to be an extroverted Coach Phil to be a wonderful and impactful coach to these kids and their families. During season two of coaching with my sister, Laura, Ryan, Phillip, and I all had the wild idea that all four of us taking on coaching at the same time would be a good idea. Phillip and Ryan coached Riley's YMCA basketball league for nine- to ten-year-olds. Yes, the most introverted of all the introverts—my brother-in-law—helped Phillip coach! If Ryan can do it, if I can do it, you can, too.

Coach Pitch Minors Braves Tournament Championship Team, July 2024

CHAPTER 11

Volunteer! If I Can Do It, You Can, Too.

Right now, Amelia is in basketball, and her coach is a woman. I saw multiple women coaches at her first practice. Especially in the younger ages, many sports leagues need volunteer coaches. If you cannot see yourself as a mom coach, I hope you will inspire your husband or brothers to volunteer to coach. Being a coach's wife is fun, and you can still find many ways to help.

Here's my playbook, my cheat sheet, to coaching youth baseball. I hope it gives a starting point to others considering and heading down this journey. And if you're not ready, at least it gives you an idea of what to look for in coaches, in player time, and in not second guessing yourself when you want to advocate for your player.

This is not a set of drills, but rather a set of strategies, which I think will be more beneficial. You can look up all kinds of drills (or observe other teams') for what your little team needs to work on developing. This is a recipe that should inspire and equip you to build a stronger team week over week, and get in some wins.

In my first season, I wished I had tips and tricks all in one place. I hope you find it useful, and I wish you the best of luck on your youth sports journey!

Lesson 1: The kids learn quickly.

It's very likely your first practice is going to feel extremely rough. Some of those kids will look like they haven't picked up a ball in their lives. And maybe some of them haven't. That's OK. It's great they showed up, and it's great their parents brought them. Have patience, and remind yourself they learn quickly. Not all of them will, but don't give up on them. For some kids, it takes more reps than others. But once it clicks, the magic happens.

These kids can also pick up on the *basic* fundamentals of the game. Every first practice, so as to not embarrass the first timers, I would jog with the team starting at home plate and ask them what base it was. Have them shout, "Home plate!" Then jog with them to first base, ask them again, and have them shout it. Then jog with them to second, and so on. **This also serves as a reminder on which way to run after they hit the ball.** The first practice I ever hosted, I had one kid shout out the base. The majority looked around in confusion. By the third game, they were all running in the right direction and knew the bases. By the third season, they were all shouting the proper bases at the first practice. See? *I promise* they can learn.

Another fundamental is teaching them when to throw to what base. In a lot of tee ball leagues, they are only learning to throw to first base. When they get to their first coach pitch league, they need guidance on when to throw to another base besides first. This is also where reps come in.

Parents, you can do this by practicing with your kids at home, too. Talk through it with them, make fake bases in the backyard, and give them simple scenarios. I have had a lot of parents and single moms mention they are worried their child is too far behind to try this or that sport. There are simple ways to help teach your kids so they don't seem so new during their first season. Even watching some baseball on TV and going through why that play happened is a huge help. I know our littles have even littler attention spans, but, I promise you, they are listening and catching on.

Lesson 2: Learn their names.

Even as normal Aunt Crissy on the sidelines, I find it tough not knowing the names of the players on my niece's and nephew's teams, let alone the children on my own kids' teams! I love cheering for the kids!

As a coach, you'd better learn those names! Imagine yelling "Run home, Johnny!" to the runner on third base, but the runner on first base's name is Johnny. Now you have Johnny trying to pass all your other runners and causing mass confusion on the field. No one wants that, least of all the coach.

Phillip is not great at learning names. At his first couple of practices, he would glance over at me and mouth, "What's his name?" And I would remember to help him on the car rides home.

Some of the kids will resemble each other, and it will be tough. After one to two practices, you will be able to match their personality traits with their own names, and then you will wonder how you ever mixed those same two players up.

LESSON 3: GET HELP FROM ADDITIONAL PARENTS.

One of my first group text messages as coach was to the parents, asking who would be able to help. If you're bringing a whole new team together, this is a great way to ask for help from parents who have the time to give it. Not all do. And I get that. But by asking up front, the ones who are on the fence will raise their hand.

As a parent, this should be a non-negotiable at some point during your child's youth sports career. Of course, you don't need to offer help every single season. But if you're not up for coaching, then put some time aside to prioritize helping, especially if you notice it's needed. There were so many moms and dads throughout my coaching seasons who were such a huge help.

Even if you are a coach at a well-funded league, every coach with an assistant coach needs parent helpers. Here is a list of ways parents could and should get involved in their kid's team:

- Dugout coach
- First-base or third-base coach
- Practice stations; see Lesson 5: Reps.
- Snacks: Create the after-game snack schedule, volunteer to bring the snacks one weekend, or create a big tub for everyone to chip in at the beginning of the season and be the snack mom who brings the tub every weekend.
- Music mom (if allowed): See chapter 10.
- Catcher: I would often need a catcher during practices, someone to catch the ball and throw it back to me for efficiency in reps.
- Parent runners during practice scrimmages
- End-of-year party: Offer up cost-effective ideas, bring

cupcakes, offer to chip in for end-of-season gifts for the players, etc. (If you have the savvy, custom baseball cards for your players are soooo cute!)

- Score keeper if needed (some leagues do this, some don't).
- Field set-up: In every league I have learned about, the leagues need help with the fields, whether it's regular upkeep or fixing them up from rain, mowing, chalking, etc. I am confident they would love your help!

LESSON 4: SHORT SAYINGS ARE EASY FOR THE PLAYERS TO REMEMBER AND PUT INTO PLAY.

I picked up on many sayings over season one and also thought of my own, realizing they were helpful.

Some of my favorite sayings, especially for the younger, newer kids, are:

- **Crab Walk**: Getting them to squat and put their gloves on the ground moving back and forth—teaches them how to field the ball and get into baseball ready positions.
- **Gator Chomp:** Teaches them to use two hands and cover the ball when fielding with their non-glove hand so they don't miss.
- **Race to the Base:** Teaches them to move quickly whether they are the runner or the fielder. It reminds them that whoever gets to the base first wins the race. This helps make them run faster.
- **They're quick, but we're quicker:** I would use this a lot when I noticed the other team's fielders were quick-fielding the ball to get the runner out at first. It would inspire the runners to run faster to first.

Here are some additional sayings you can use for the younger crew—I saw a lot of success when using these:

- Watch the ball *the whole way* (or: See the ball, hit the ball). This makes them understand the importance of not taking their eyes off the ball.
- Hit it to center field (this actually works quite a bit). If you have a player who notoriously is hitting hard fouls, try saying to them, "Hit it to center!" Or "Hit it back at Coach!" This often helps them redirect by looking and taking a quick focus on their target. And often you'll get a chuckle at telling them to hit their coach.

Lesson 5: Reps, reps, reps, reps, reps, reps, reps, reps.

(Anyone else read the title of this lesson and fist pump their hands in the air to the tune of LMFAO and Lil' Jon's song, "shots, shots, shots, shots, shots, shots!" Just me?)

Coach David taught me about reps at the first coaches meeting, and thank goodness for that! Teaching these kids how to play the game means absolutely nothing if you don't teach them the skills of catching, throwing, fielding, and hitting first. And, just like me throwing nearly one hundred pop-ups to Aiden on the day before his game-winning pop-up catch, doing reps ensures you're less likely to make a mistake in the game.

Help your player find joy in the reps. Some players will naturally prefer catching over hitting, or vice versa. For instance, Dylan loves to hit. I know that is common for his age, but there are kids who would let me throw pop-ups to them all day if I could. So if Dylan did extra reps for fielding grounders and catching, then I would reward him an extra bucket in hitting. I would find what the players liked to do and try to reward them after they worked on something they didn't love to do as much.

Hitting: If you have a real beginner at hitting, someone whose swing is completely off (swinging up to down), **get them on a tee.** You can send your weakest batters with them to that station and have them hit on the tee over and over. Make sure a parent or a coach is there helping them. Give them extra hitting time in practice. That's not to say your strongest hitters shouldn't hit on a tee, that's just to say you may have other skills you want those players to focus on—like fielding or pop-up catching.

Whichever skill you need that player to work on the most, start them out at that station. That way, if you run out of time, they got in the reps they needed before you practice fielding as a team, or scrimmaging.

Parents—do reps with your kids at home! The *Sandlot* days are over. We can bring them back! You can also make a game out of the reps.

When Dylan was seven, I knew he could catch the ball more consistently than he was doing during the season. He did not love reps for playing catch. But we started taking him outside and throwing the ball to him. He got bored a little easily, and he would get frustrated that I, specifically, would tell him he could do better. He was straight up letting the balls fall out of his glove. It started to drive me bonkers! So I said to him, "For every five balls you catch, I'll give you $1. If you let the ball fall out of your glove, that's minus $1." Within twenty minutes of catch and throw, I owed him $3, and he was doing much better at catching consistently. Your reward might be treats, minutes of screentime, etc.—and your reps may be different than catch and throw.

If you remember back in chapter six, I took Dylan outside and vowed to never strike him out again. We didn't need any reward or system for those reps. He absolutely loved it. The kid loves to hit. Once I started getting a little more scared of pitching to him, I wouldn't pitch as many buckets to him, and there were a couple times he would say, "Come on, Mom, one more bucket!!" Even if you are the biggest fan of baseball, you may not love every single aspect of it or every single skill it takes to be great. That's OK!

Last quick story I'll leave you with for reps—Coach David told us Camden would hit one hundred to one hundred and fifty balls before every one of his high school baseball games. That stuck with me. Wow, OK, so warming up before a game is a good thing. It builds up your stamina and gets you in good habits for when you're up at bat. It made me wonder why didn't I do more reps when I pitched for softball in high school (OK, Crissy, this book isn't about *your* softball journey.)

If you have one hour for practice, do thirty minutes of reps, then a thirty-minute scrimmage.

Lesson 6: Clean-up hitters? Yes and no.

It depends on your league's rules and strategy. Think through this, and pay attention to how your hitters are doing. When you put several of your better hitters toward the front, they get more opportunities to hit in the game. Not too close to the front, because you want them to hit your base hitters home for maximum runs.

Does your league's rules allow you to go through the batting line-up if there aren't three outs? Make sure you ask how many players the opposing team has before the game begins. If they have eleven players, and you only had nine show up, your best two batters should be the first batters because if you get to bat around, you get to bat them twice.

If you have the same amount of players as your opposing team, then this is your ideal line-up:

1. Solid Batter
2. Solid Batter
3. Better/OK Batter
4. Strongest Batter
5. Weaker Batter
6. Solid Batter
7. Weaker Batter
8. Solid Batter
9. Weaker/OK Batter
10. Second or Third Strongest Batter

Don't just willy nilly put together a batting line-up without paying attention to how your players are at-bat.

Explain to the strong batters why they are the clean-up hitters and what that means. A lot of the players love to be first at-bat, but I would always pull the last at-bat or the fourth batter aside and explain to them why they were there. They were not last because they weren't good—quite the opposite. Then we explained to them how many runs they brought in by being that last batter, and they ended up loving it.

Still, as amazing as you make clean-up hitter sound, those batters are also going to want to score during some games. The clean-up hitter may get two to three runs in every time, but unless they are a home run hitter, they are not scoring themselves. Make sure you shake up the batting line-up from time to time if you notice that happening so they can score runs, too. This scenario, however, is only likely to happen if the opposing team never gets three outs on your team.

Another little trick I have is putting your most trusted batter first. Not only the kid you know is going to hit it solid every time and motivate the players behind them, but the kid who gets up to bat with a smile on their face and makes you feel comfortable on the pitcher's mound. It starts the game out with positive momentum. There were many times I would have an exhale of relief when certain batters got up to home plate. I found it important to put them around the batters that would often strike out. It would keep the momentum going.

Lesson 7: The kids must hit.

You're more capable of pitching than you give yourself credit for. Get there early, or stay late. Your goal is to get the ball over the plate. What they need at this age is the confidence of hitting the ball.

If your players don't hit, you will not win a game. Heck, there really won't be a game in the six-to-seven age group.

Here are some practical tips:

- Don't throw heat; aim to get it over the plate.
- For weak swings from the batter, aim for where they are swinging, not in the strike zone.
- If a batter is not swinging straight across, get them on a tee A LOT.
- Get a lot of hitting reps in those first few practices, learn where your hitters swing, and pitch the ball there. I cannot

stress this enough. You should have a field-and-throw station going on while the pitcher is constantly pitching to the players. Learn your batters to help them hit at the plate. You can remind them of what they learned when they get up there.

- Make them comfortable at the plate during game time. Smile at them, ask them if they are ready to have some fun, and make the opposing team work for it. You get them to smile, they let their guard down and become less nervous.

- To develop your more talented hitters, use wiffle balls, weighted balls, and tennis balls. The goal is for them to find the ball with their bat and build up their strength in their swing.

- Back elbow up—if your tiny player out there is closed up tight in their swing, they won't hit. Tell them to get their elbow up—Phillip recognized this in many young players and always corrected them—**and then they hit.**

- If you're a terrible pitcher and just can't get it over the plate, find someone else (or practice more!). Don't be prideful. Your players hitting that ball is more important than your ego.

- Some parents/dads are better at developing a player's swing. Listen to them, and get advice from them. The elbow up comes from Phillip. The "squish the bug" comes from David. I can't develop a player's swing for the life of me. But I can get them to hit. And I believe that is more important at six to seven years old—but you don't want them creating bad habits if they are showing talent.

LESSON 8: BONUS PRACTICES ARE A MUST.

Y'all, I love me a bonus practice!

Again, this is dependent on your league's rules, but most of the leagues in our area allow extra time to get together with your players. I find it important to call it a bonus practice because it's possible not all parents can get their kid to extra practices, but you definitely want all of your players together for practice at least once a week. So if they are going to come for a practice, you want it to be the main practice.

Bonus practices can be a bit more fun depending on who from your team shows up. Perhaps the scrimmages are a bit longer—which the kids love—or maybe you do more hitting with them. It all depends on what you need to work on based on how your official practice went.

This is also a great bonding time, a time to execute fun games with the players so they are simply having a blast together.

A great bonus practice is scrimmaging and aiming to hit "dingers" or "home runs." The quotes are for a reason—a nearby tee ball field to practice on is always great for this, an unofficial field so you can draw the "home run" zone yourself. Any player who hits it in the home-run zone gets to run and be cheered on the whole way.

While it may not be an official home run, it motivates the kids to hit it harder and farther and cheer for each other. We've had several of those for bonus practices.

You can use bonus practices to rep pop-ups or try out different plays. Get the parents involved in base running so the kids get used to fielding with each other and getting outs. Kids love nothing more than getting their parents or siblings out. Have those parents run fast. Then the kids get used to faster runners and aren't shocked when one of the teams is loaded with Usain Bolts.

Lesson 9: Rewards go a long way.

I love rewarding kids. I teach my kids that in real life you get rewarded, too. Do a great job at work? Get promoted. Or, you don't, and you get fired. Work hard at learning a skill like changing the oil in your car? Reward! You save time and money—and you look awesome in front of your friends. Life is a reward system.

Bringing popsicles, lollipops, treats, baseball trading cards, and Pokémon cards to practice from time to time is a great way to reinforce hard work paying off. It doesn't have to be expensive, and it certainly shouldn't be every single practice, but it does go a long way.

One time, we were neck and neck in the last inning, and I told the players, "If you get these runs and we win this game, we will have popsicles after our next practice." Well, it's a good thing we won that game, because I didn't have a back-up plan if they didn't win! But it worked—they got motivated and refocused, and Coach Laura threw ice pops into a cooler with tons of ice for after practice one day.

Lesson 10: Learn the rules, and ask questions.

Don't suffer in silence. Understand the rules, and, if you don't understand them, ask questions. You don't have to know all the rules like the back of your hand for volunteer coaching, but you should put some time into reading the rulebook. You will and should learn as you go.

Once you get on the field, ask questions. Ask the director if something went funny in the game that you didn't understand

Lesson 11: Team bonding for the win.

This is the time to start showing the players what it means to be a teammate. Sometimes opportunities present themselves where you can do team outings, maybe there is a one-day baseball camp happening, or a local minors or college baseball game where you can get group tickets/discounts or even free tickets for all, or potentially a team park day. During one season, Phillip sent an email to our local minor league and was able to not only get free tickets for all our players and their parents, but also for their siblings! It was a wonderful way to start the season off together and to welcome the new players into the team. It never hurts to ask.

It can be smaller, like celebrating teammates' birthdays. Offer to bring cupcakes for a teammate if it's their birthday or sing happy birthday in a huddle or at home plate for birthdays. The players feel special that their teams celebrate them, even if it's with a song.

If a team experience outside of games and practices isn't an option, or you simply don't have the time to make it happen, that is completely OK. Teaching players about being good teammates can happen in the everyday moments you already have. It shows up in the way they cheer for each other at-bat, how they support one another from the dugout, and how they celebrate a great play with a high five or a big smile. Those small moments add up, and, over time, they teach kids what it means to be part of a team and just how special that can feel.

LESSON 12: RANDOM TIPS FROM AN UNDEFEATED VOLUNTEER COACH

- **Gloves:** Until about age seven or eight, gloves are really tricky to get right. Get the size a smidge bigger than tee ball gloves for coach pitch. Anything bigger and it won't fit. Too small and it won't have a big enough wingspan to get the ball. This is why it's tricky. Then: **Break. It. In.** Glove oil you can buy anywhere helps. Spray it, put a baseball inside of the glove, wrap rubber bands around it, and sit on it. Put it under a couch cushion. Do whatever you need to do to break it in; that will give your player the best shot at catching and fielding.

- **Ages five to eight:** Put your best players at first and pitcher and rep, rep, rep. It might go without saying, but, of course, put your best catcher at first base. If you don't have a player who is great at catching the ball yet, put the kid who has the best handle on using their glove at first. Don't put a kid with a tee ball glove at first. There's not enough room for them to catch the ball in that little glove. If they can't catch yet, but they are decent at fielding, enough balls will go toward first that they can field it and tag out at first.

  - You're going to be tempted to put your best player at shortstop. Don't do it. I repeat: Don't do it. There have been so many games where I have whispered to Phillip, "If that shortstop was at first base instead, that would be three outs already." If they can field, at least at first base, there is the base to get an out. At shortstop, the skills of themselves and the other players have to go beyond fielding and stepping on a base. The shortstop then has to decide where to go. Second? First? Then accurately throw it to first, then the first baseman has to catch it. But you put your best player at shortstop, so first baseman is likely not going to catch it.

- ◦ Why is first and pitcher a great strategy at this age? Most of these players are not hitting the ball past the pitcher. You might have two to four strong hitters on the opposing team who will consistently get the ball to the outfield or to second/third baseline. The rest of them are going right there in the pitcher's mound area. Once it clicks, it is chef's kiss! You'll be thanking me! Then, your kids will start to feel like real ball players getting some outs, and the whole team will get more motivated.

- ◦ Once you've selected your first base and pitcher, have them practice over and over again. Get them to be buddies. Dylan and Miles ultimately came up with a handshake all on their own—do I even need to tell you how incredibly adorable it was watching a six- and seven-year-old create their hand shake (insert heart eye emoji here)? No, I don't have to tell you. This is a duo you can create—don't skip out on it.

- **Injuries:** Injuries are tough. These are small kids, and you don't want any of them to get hurt. It can be scary. BUT most injuries are minor and won't be thought of five minutes later. Remember that. Aim to have the player shake it off first. Maybe they get hit in the knee playing the catcher position, but don't immediately send them to the dugout to switch them out. Give them a moment, encourage them to shake it off. I've seen kids who I really didn't think had it in them shake it off.

If you're a mom like me, and it makes you feel better, pack all the things: water wipes, Aquaphor, cool Band-Aids, ice packs, gauze. You know the list goes on and on. It's nice to be the mom who always has something. Sometimes, it's easier to have these things on-hand than to use the first aid kits that are provided. Even a water wipe to clean off a boo-boo can make them *feel* better and ready to get back out there.

And finally, Toughen The Players Up A Bit!

I've thought a lot about how I wanted to end this book. Baseball and youth sports need to be fun, and every kid should feel included. I've had multiple conversations at home about how the player, the child, is not at fault for how he is being raised at home or taught to conduct himself on the field. When they come to play their sport, it should be a blast. It should make them want to continue to play sports and try new sports and learn to make friends.

It should also be a tool for them to learn some adversity. I recently went to one of Riley's volleyball games, and her team was playing a team they were clearly more skilled than—except, Riley's team was losing. Riley's team all had a look of apathy on their faces. Almost like deer in headlights. Going through the motions of the game, but not playing like they could. Finally, the volleyball coach shouted sternly, "GET IT TOGETHER. TURN IT AROUND RIGHT NOW" while pointing her finger in a circle motion at all of them, and then pointing down when she said, "RIGHT NOW."

Immediately, the girls' demeanors changed. There were more smiles on their faces, more focused looks, and the ball was getting hit harder. They ended up coming back to score more but lost that game. Then, in the final third set, first to fifteen, they only let the other team score four, and they ultimately won the series.

Sometimes, you need to be stern, even with six-year-olds. They need to be told to stop playing in the dirt. They need to run laps or sit in the dugout for a few minutes if they are kicking dirt or talking back often. It's OK to tell a player you know they can do better, they can run faster—because you've seen it from them before! Help them reach their full potential, and don't settle for less. They need to learn to accept feedback for the real world. Teach them to reach for excellence. Tell them to play at home. Independently toss the ball in their glove, run a few laps in the backyard. I guess what I am saying is, tough love can be fun, too. As I mentioned earlier in my memoir, being good and winning *is* fun. Sometimes, tough love is part of that.

Above all, get out there and volunteer. And just as we want to teach our players excellence, aim to reach for excellence in your volunteering, too! Fill youth sports leagues with more slightly obsessed and well-meaning coaches like Coach Laura, Coach Phil, and me.

I've learned about many youth sports' leagues since I started on this journey, and coaches are always needed, not only at the Y. Always. Sports programs aim to hold on tight to their great volunteers. They are tough to come by, but it doesn't have to be like that. Volunteer, and then care at least a little bit about winning, because if you care even a little bit, you will be a great volunteer to those kids. We only have one life to live after all, why not make the most of this time with your kids?

When I'm sitting outside the pearly gates, hopefully years and years from now, I won't be able to say much about what good I did in God's Kingdom. But helping His children learn to love their teammates and inspiring their passion for life through sports, well, that I know I will be able to say. Laura calls our time volunteering one of her "tickets into heaven." And all I'm saying is—it can be something you add to your pearly gates resume, too.